SOCIAL WORK, POLITICS AND SOCIETY

From radicalism to orthodoxy

Kenneth McLaughlin

This edition published in Great Britain in 2008 by

The Policy Press
University of Bristol
Fourth Floor
Beacon House
Queen's Road
Bristol BS8 1QU
UK

Tel +44 (0)117 331 4054
Fax +44 (0)117 331 4093
e-mail tpp-info@bristol.ac.uk
www.policypress.org.uk

British Library Cataloguing in Publication Data
A catalogue record for this book is available from the British Library.

Library of Congress Cataloging-in-Publication Data
A catalog record for this book has been requested.

ISBN 978 1 84742 044 2 paperback
ISBN 978 1 84742 045 9 hardcover

Cover design by In-Text Design, Bristol
Front cover: image kindly supplied by www.alamy.com
Printed and bound in Great Britain by Hobbs the Printers, Southampton

Contents

Acknowledgements

My thanks to all who have commented on earlier drafts and provided much-needed advice and critical comments, most of which I took on board, some of which I did not, all of which I considered valuable: Janet Batsleer, Erica Burman, Debra Hayes, Dave Edmondson, James Heartfield, Mike Fitzpatrick, Sue Jones, Mary Langan, Ian Parker, Malcolm Payne, Liz Pell, Sam Price, Debbie Thackray, Chris Yianni. Thanks also to those at The Policy Press who advised at various stages of the book's production: Philip de Bary, Karen Bowler, Leila Ebrahimi, Jacqueline Lawless, Jo Morton and Emily Watt.

In the course of this book, I have reproduced short extracts from some of my earlier work: 'Stressing vulnerability: stress discourse in the public sector', (2004) *Journal of Critical Psychology, Counselling and Psychotherapy*, vol 4, no 4, pp 223-41 (by permission of PCCS Books Ltd); 'From ridicule to institutionalisation: anti-oppression, the state and social work', (2005) *Critical Social Policy*, vol 25, no 3, pp 283-305, © Critical Social Policy Ltd (by permission of Sage Publications Ltd); 'Revisiting the public/private divide: theoretical, political and personal implications of their unification', (2007) *Practice*, vol 19, no 4, pp 241-53, www.informaworld.com (by permission of Taylor and Francis); 'Regulation and risk in social work: The General Social Care Council and Social Care Register in context', *British Journal of Social Work*, vol 37, pp 1263-77.

Introduction

Most of us, at some point in our lives will have contact with social services. This may be directly, as a user of social services, as a carer for such a recipient, as a result of working in a related profession, or indirectly through conversation or media representation. Whichever the case may be, each of us will probably harbour some ideas, prejudices and misconceptions of who social workers are and what they do.

While all communities have informal and formal arrangements for looking after their members, for the purpose of this book it is when such care becomes organised at a wider, societal level that it becomes social work. In this sense, social work is seen not as an activity dating back to antiquity, but as one originating in the seventeenth century, and developing more comprehensively in the mid-eighteenth to nineteenth centuries within the changing socio-economic and intellectual currents of that time. This interaction continued to influence the development of social work throughout the twentieth century and is no less important today. The aim of this book is to identify such societal influences on contemporary social policy and social work.

My primary concern is not with the minutiae of social work intervention; there is already a plethora of material addressing this. Practical application, so far as it is discussed, is from the point of view of the way in which wider societal and political influences can affect the course of the intervention. Nevertheless, my experience as a social work practitioner has greatly influenced me in undertaking this project.

Working in a statutory mental health team I became aware that in my team's locality we had seen a gradual increase in the number of compulsory admissions to hospital under the 1983 Mental Health Act. Some further research discovered that this was not confined to us, but was indicative of a national trend. Because these developments have implications for mental health workers and service users, I was interested in discovering what lay behind this rise in admissions, especially as it coincided with increased public and governmental concern with the supposed threat posed by psychiatric patients, and which has led to the introduction of the 2007 Mental Health Act.

Similarly, I could not help but notice how many seemingly progressive and benign developments such as speech and behaviour codes were more and more often being used as a way of disciplining the workforce, stifling debate and formalising interpersonal interactions. Informal relationships were increasingly viewed with suspicion, with more formal relationships with authority presented as more benevolent. Another defining moment happened at a meeting. I was part of the steering group for a centre set up to provide people with an alternative to hospital admission when their mental state was poor. The service was a success, and did indeed seem to fill a previous gap in service provision for those in acute need. This centre, buoyed by its success, then decided to set up a telephone helpline for those who, while not at an acute crisis stage, nevertheless required someone to talk to. The rationale was that such early intervention would prevent further deterioration and subsequent need for professional intervention.

After a three-month trial run, the next meeting of the steering group reviewed this new service. It transpired that hardly anyone was using it. In fact, a high percentage of the calls received were from someone I had referred. If his calls were excluded, the number of calls, already very few, would have been minimal. It was decided that we should list possible reasons for the lack of take-up of the service. Suggestions included that perhaps the helpline was open at the wrong hours, and when people needed most help, for example in the middle of the night, the helpline was closed. Perhaps, not enough people were aware of its existence, so therefore leaflets could be produced and placed in doctors' surgeries, supermarkets, buses and so on. In addition, we could approach local radio stations and ask them to publicise the service.

Each suggestion, to my mind, was entirely plausible. However, what struck me was that not once did anyone consider it possible that perhaps they were not needed. Two things were noticeable. First, this echoed with Dineen's (1999) point that the mental health industry was like any other. To survive, it had to expand, find new markets (by discovering hitherto hidden illnesses or syndromes) and present itself as the solution to these problems. Second, the underlying assumption of the steering committee seemed to be that the public could not cope without their professional input. The possibility that perhaps the majority of the public could manage quite adequately without them was simply not considered. It is this professional arrogance, which – while never admitted – reveals a real contempt for the public's ability to cope without them, that for me underlies much of contemporary social policy and practice.

This book explores the history of social work in the United Kingdom in such a way as to identify problematic areas of current social policy and practice. It acknowledges past influences on the subject of social work and is concerned with identifying such trends today. Historically, the theoretical underpinnings and practical application of professional social work has been influenced by prevailing social mores, and has, in turn, influenced professional and societal views of the subjects of such intervention. In recent years, most notably from the 1970s onwards, there has been increasing recognition of this by social theorists, policy makers and political activists (including those who use or are subject to social services). This is not to give the impression that social work, in the form of the workers, policy makers and latterly service users, has passively absorbed such ideas and changes. On the contrary, the profession's contribution to policy and practice is highlighted in order to show the interactive nature of political, social and professional change. It is for this reason that a historical and dialectical approach is used; societal and intellectual trends are shown to have influenced the development of the social work profession, and, albeit to a lesser extent, social work has influenced such developments in society.

My contention is that, despite the rhetoric of empowerment that pervades the social work literature, underlying many of the developments within both social work and social policy is a more atavistic view of humanity. The present epoch is one of 'diminished subjectivity' (Heartfield, 2002), where people in general, and social work clients in particular, are seen more as 'objects' than 'subjects', as simultaneously weak, vulnerable and potentially dangerous.

Manifestations of diminished subjectivity include a risk-averse culture where the 'precautionary principle' dominates; a therapeutic turn in which ever more human interactions are viewed through a psychological prism, with people more often seen as in need of third-party professional intervention; a distrust of informal relationships, which are held to be sites of abuse; and a political culture that lacks vision and instead is focused on the micromanagement of human behaviour. Social work is the arena where contemporary politics is increasingly played out, and where policies and practices that undermine human subjectivity are ubiquitous. It is therefore important to understand the reasons behind this and the implications for social workers, their clients and the wider public.

Of course, social work, as a mode of state/professional intervention in social and individual life has always been political. This political aspect may have been relatively unacknowledged in the early stages of social work's development but it was brought to the fore by the radical social work movement and its offshoots from the 1970s onwards. This politicising of social work, important as it was at the time, is not so helpful today. Contemporary social work has been subjected to a particular form of politicisation at a time when politics has shifted onto the terrain, and adopted the techniques, of social work. In other words, social work today is overly politicised while politics is overly concerned with social work.

There is relatively little criticism of these developments, and much of what there is tends to miss the point. Critics from the Right decry the overt politicisation of social work, denouncing the latest manifestation of what they see as 'political correctness gone mad', while those on the Left will argue that since the heady radical days of the 1970s and 1980s there has been a steady decline of radicalism in social work, and that there is a need to revive the traditions of radical social work. What both sides often fail to recognise is that ideas and practices associated with both radical social work and political correctness are no longer marginal but have been incorporated into the mainstream of British political life. The belief that British society is inherently racist is no longer the preserve of left-wing radicals; it is now commonplace. And, though few would subscribe to the radical feminist idea that all acts of heterosexual sex equate to rape, the belief that relationships are inherently abusive is a guiding principle behind many government pronouncements – for example, that midwives should routinely ask pregnant women whether they are being abused by their partner (Hehir, 2004).

There has also been a 'therapeutic turn' in political life, with feelings and emotions being central to many government initiatives, from measures to combat stress to those aimed at raising the self-esteem of the populace. The state and its agencies are increasingly concerned with helping us along the road to psychological fulfilment.

Techniques used in social work, such as counselling, have also been increasingly incorporated into the mainstream of government policy and organisational culture. Workplace counsellors are increasingly replacing trade unions as the bridge between the worker and management. Unions themselves have played a pivotal role in allowing a therapeutic culture into the workplace, in the process portraying their members as weak and/or abusive and in need of support and/or censure. Themes such as empowerment and the micromanagement of human interaction have become dominant today and are no longer confined to the relationship between care professional and client. On the contrary, they have become institutionalised in both our culture and subjectivity.

The therapeutic turn in politics and the politicisation of social work have also led to a redrawing of, or at its most extreme a failure to recognise any, boundaries between the public/private, personal/political, sickness/health. However flawed such dichotomies can be, the collapse of any distinction also has major implications for our individual subjectivity and collective humanity.

Social work has been criticised for the way in which it can merely help people cope with their problems rather than transcend them. Today, a similar charge can be made against the wider body politic. The 1980s and 1990s saw a major shift away from the more traditional political battleground around economics and industrial relations towards more lifestyle issues, for example around AIDS, teenage pregnancy, school meals, interpersonal abuse, obesity, parenting, bullying (in schools and work), anti-social behaviour, smoking and drinking. Bereft of political vision as to how to overcome political problems, the government is taking on the role of social worker, helping us to cope with difficulties in our private lives. Social work may be political but politics should not be about social work.

This book sets these trends in their wider historical and political context, identifying influences on the development of social work and politics in order to trace the roots of such a degraded view of those subject to social work, social workers themselves and society in general.

As will be seen, there is no consensus as to what actually constitutes social work, and even where there is some broad agreement on the role of the social worker, there are still many overlaps with other professions both inside and outside the social care field. The very proposition that social work is itself a profession is also disputed, and the governing body of the 'profession', the General Social Care Council, has, as part of its remit under the 2000 Care Standards Act, the task of pursuing steps to clarify and register just who exactly is entitled to call themselves a 'social worker' (DH, 2000b) and to define their roles and tasks in a changing world (Blewett et al, 2007).

The desire to clarify and create a distinct identity is in part a response to a fear that social work is being subsumed within other disciplines. Social work, particularly today, cannot be seen in isolation from other professions or institutions. With the rise of the 'multidisciplinary', 'multi-agency' team, social workers are to be found in ever-increasing areas of life (Parton and O'Byrne, 2000). Therefore, at times, guidance and legislation specifically aimed at other staff – for example in the health service – is used to highlight aspects of my argument since it affects social workers who are employed by, or in contact with, such services.

As such, a broad approach to the subject is adopted throughout; social work is ever changing, and ever expanding into areas of life that were once not seen as within its remit. Such a statement would probably not ring true to anyone involved with, for example, statutory child protection or mental health work, which are often viewed as the frontline and most demanding areas of social work practice, services in which staff shortages and scarce resources can lead to only those deemed most 'high risk' being given a service. Nevertheless, social workers are not confined to such areas, in recent years becoming involved in the less overtly coercive aspects of the role, around such issues as school bullying, 'healthy living' and anti-social behaviour initiatives. With its commitment, in principle at least, to fight inequality and oppression, social work is also charged with challenging 'racist', 'sexist' or other discriminatory words or actions. In this respect, it is argued that social work is part of a trend towards enforcing a new moral code of behaviour on society in general, and its clientele in particular.

Readers should not, as they go from chapter to chapter, conclude that I see no place for social work or social workers in society. Children, for whatever reason, whether through parental neglect or their carers' premature or accidental death, will need alternative places to live. Likewise, whether as a result of mental or physical frailty, many people will require services to improve their quality of life. 'Social work', as an activity, has always existed, and it would be a poor indictment of society if we were to lose the capacity to care for those in need of assistance. This book, therefore, is not 'anti social work', rather it is critical of contemporary manifestations of social work, which, it is contended, are reflective of a wider sense of societal pessimism and mistrust that is ultimately destructive. In this respect it is aspects of the overt politicisation and professionalisation of social work that are seen as problematic.

The areas investigated were chosen for a number of reasons. Not only did they have to be issues of interest to some professionals and academics, they also had to have influenced social policy and the social work profession's training and practice requirements. In addition, my interest was in the influence of the changing direction of left-wing political thought on contemporary debates, and of the role of activists in framing their demands and influencing policy makers.

Given the vast scope of activity that is carried out under the name of 'social work', there are of course many trends and influences that will not be covered extensively. For example, some writers would argue that issues such as the drive towards managerialism, or the purchaser/ provider split of the 1990s, are major influences on current service provision (eg Cowen, 1999; Lloyd, 2002). While these are discussed briefly, my main aim is to identify what I consider to be a relatively unconsidered aspect of current theory, policy and practice, namely the anti-human sentiments that have crept insidiously into the debate and also into how we view and interact with each other. Therefore the more technical areas of practice associated with the new managerialism are not considered as relevant as the chosen topics of anti-oppression, stress, risk and vulnerability. The chosen areas are also more relevant to an investigation into subjectivity than the technical, procedural areas of service delivery.

Chapters One, Two and Three situate the book in terms of the historical development of social work and social theory. The focus is on developments within a United Kingdom, particularly an English, context, although influences from further afield are discussed where relevant. Chapter One details the history of social work from its origins in the Poor Laws of the seventeenth century and the charitable organisations of the eighteenth and nineteenth centuries, to the development of social work through to the mid-twentieth century. The incorporation of the 'psy' disciplines of psychiatry, psychology and psychoanalysis into social work theory and practice not only provides insight into the development of the profession, but is useful in that the criticisms levelled against this incorporation appear relatively muted today, when arguably the 'psy-complex' is more pronounced. Reasons for this are elaborated on in the following chapters. My aim is to give the reader an understanding of the roots of social work and also to highlight how wider societal and political issues were crucial to the trajectory of its development.

The main theme of Chapter Two is the politicising of social work from the 1970s onwards, from the class-based critique of the radical social work movement to the influence of feminist and anti-racist writers, to the contribution to the debates and practices from disability activists as well as gay and lesbian campaigners. The influence of such perspectives on social work training and development is also highlighted.

In Chapter Three the reaction to such developments is discussed. The assumption among many of the proponents of anti-racist/anti-oppressive practice that there has been a sustained backlash against their project is contested. It is argued that what were seen at the time as radical, progressive movements were in fact the outcome of political defeat, and in the intervening years they have become institutionalised in ways that are problematic. Anti-racist/anti-oppressive social workers, rather than being an empowering force combating inequality, on the contrary may find themselves at the forefront of enforcing a new moral code of behaviour on the public, themselves and their clientele.

The remainder of the book then discusses closely related areas where contemporary views of the subject are revealing, and where social work has influenced, and been influenced by, such a degraded view of humanity; the rise of pathology and abuse, the contemporary preoccupation with risk and vulnerability and the focus on stress and bullying within the workplace.

The exponential rise of diagnostic criteria and proliferation of the concept of abuse is therefore the subject of Chapter Four. A brief history of psychiatry and psychology allows us to see not only how such disciplines were influenced by factors external to them, but also how ever more areas of life became subject to a medical gaze and interpretation. Related to this, the notion that interpersonal relations, rather than being a source of strength and respite could be sites of abuse became increasingly popular. This diagnostic and abuse expansion becomes somewhat self-fulfilling, each apparently fuelling the other. Of interest to social work is not only the incorporation of a quasi-medical framework, but also its role in constructing the subject of abuse. The main point is not to dispute that in some relations instances of abuse take place; such a proposition, especially for anyone involved in social work, where such instances are encountered, would be unsustainable. Rather, the point is that as an overarching cultural viewpoint, the discourse of abuse is revealing in what it says about contemporary professional attitudes to the general public.

The next three chapters focus on the subject of risk in social work. However, it is not the attempts at creating 'risk-assessment tools' that are of primary interest, but the prevailing climate of fear that views the contemporary subject as one who is at risk. Three discourses of risk pertaining to social work are identified: social workers as assessors of risk; social workers as at risk; and social workers as a risk. How these three discourses affect not only social workers but also carry implications for service users is highlighted.

Chapter Five focuses directly on statutory mental health social work, particularly in relation to the contemporary concern with risk management and risk minimisation. Social work here is seen as having a primary role in the assessment of risk. By discussing the wider societal preoccupation with risk avoidance, its incorporation into social policy and social work can be highlighted, providing a clear example of where social work practice cannot be divorced from wider societal trends. A new Mental Health Act (DH, 2007) that amends the 1983 Act has been influenced, to a large extent, by high-profile tragedies where psychiatric patients have killed themselves or others. By discussing the actual threat posed by such people, it can be shown that the fear outweighs the reality of danger, and the dangers to civil liberties inherent in the proposed changes can be highlighted. While, as will be seen, such concerns have been the focus of much debate in the mental health field, this chapter also highlights the increase in coercive measures by social workers under the 1983 Mental Health Act. It is proposed that this rise is no coincidence and that the societal trend for a 'safety first' approach has been adopted in practice, to the possible disadvantage of service users.

In Chapter Six, though still concerned with the issue of mental health, we move away from such a specific area of statutory social work intervention towards one that may be less overt, but is arguably more insidious and more revealing about how we relate to adversity and each other: the subject of stress. Whereas the previous chapter's focus concerned a relatively small section of society, the 'stress epidemic' is held to be universal, affecting everyone and virtually every social situation. In this discourse, the social worker is not positioned as an assessor of risk, but as at risk.

The chapter therefore discusses the rise of the stress phenomenon but, rather than viewing it as evidence of a rise in mental 'illness', sees it as a discursive construct rooted in changing sociopolitical conditions. The influence of this discourse on social work is discussed, not only at the level of direct social work input but at an academic and institutional level whereby interpretations of, and reactions to, a wide variety of personal, social and work-related situations are formed and mediated. In addition, links to the preceding chapters are evident, in that the rise of pathological diagnoses, categorisations of abuse and the concept of the 'at risk' individual are all implicated as causes of 'stress'.

From social workers as assessors of, and subject to, risk, Chapter Seven identifies a third and more recent trend, that of social workers themselves as being viewed as a risk. This is done by highlighting the increasing trend towards statutory control and regulation of the profession, in particular the setting up of the general social care councils, the drive towards registration of the social care workforce, and associated codes of conduct for employers and employees involved in social care. Such measures, invariably presented as necessary to prevent the abuse of the vulnerable, entail a vast increase in the surveillance and regulation of a substantial number of the workforce of the country, both in work and outside work. It is argued that the relative lack of criticism of what are unprecedented regulatory measures is reflective of a society and a profession that are acutely sensitive to perceived dangers, and where there is a presumption that we cannot trust anyone, including those who should care for us.

Chapter Eight revisits the relationship between politics and social work. In untangling the complexities of the politicisation of social work and its consequences, I argue that in many respects the debate misses a more fundamental problem. Focusing on the extent to which social work is political obscures the fact that, in contemporary society, politics has become social work. Intervening in the minutiae of individuals' lives has long been the concern of social work in its various guises. Increasingly, though, the state, via health and social care initiatives, is encroaching ever further into this terrain.

To conclude, I consider some proposals by writers also concerned by the state of contemporary social work, pointing out that many of the problems we currently face in social work and the wider political arena have been influenced by people within the social work profession. Working with individuals with different experiences, who may be vulnerable, at risk or a risk, is a fact for social workers. Extrapolating from such cases to wider society is, however, not only inaccurate but dangerous and demeaning. Today, the perception of people as being vulnerable, at risk or potentially dangerous is ubiquitous. Social work has not only been influenced by these developments, but has also contributed to present-day views of the human subject. Instead of contributing to such a situation, social work is called upon to mount a more robust defence of the subject and of the human potential.

ONE

Understandings of and developments within social work

The need for social work

If social work is seen as an attempt to help people who are in need, and human beings are seen as naturally social and empathetic, then it could be argued that social work is an extension of our natural humanity. This was the view favoured by the Association of Directors of Social Services (ADSS) in 1982, who acknowledged that social care has always existed, being done by friends, family, neighbours and volunteers. For the ADSS, 'a civilized society could not survive without the concrete expression of goodwill in myriad ways by the vast majority of the profession' (1982, p 1). According to them, social workers are necessary only for those whose problems 'require the application of knowledge or skill in a disciplined way for their solution' (ADSS, 1982, p 1).

There is, however, a more pessimistic view of the need for social workers. Far from being altruistic, this view sees human beings as inherently selfish, especially when feeling under threat. In times of conflict and/or when there are scarce resources, perhaps we are less likely to help our neighbours and more likely to ignore their plight or add to it by exploiting their weakness for our gain. In this case social work can be seen as necessary to protect the weak from the strong. Social work can therefore be seen as either a natural good, as part of our common humanity, or as a necessity to stifle the baser instincts of society, particularly in times of conflict.

There is historical evidence to support both these positions. Payne (2005) identifies three claims about the origin of social work: 1) social work originates as soon as organised helping appears; 2) social work originates in organisational responses to social changes arising from industrialisation in the late nineteenth century; 3) social work, in its twenty-first-century form originates when social work becomes incorporated within established social welfare systems.

The key phrase is that of 'organised helping', which allows us to differentiate between individual or familial help, whether of a short- or longer-term arrangement, and that of a systematic form of organisation which is characteristic of all three positions.

Developing social work

As a profession social work has its roots in the socio-economic changes of the mid-eighteenth–nineteenth centuries, a time that saw not only material changes but also changes in how opinion formers – philanthropists, charitable organisations, church groups – viewed society. At the start of the twentieth century, statute was mainly concerned with the Poor Laws and the 1890 Lunacy Act. However, these roots themselves developed from earlier medieval legislation and services. The movements were deeply influenced by Judaeo-Christian thought and ideas of charity, although social control was also evident, for example in the asylum system (Payne, 1996).

In Britain, the Protestant Reformation, the Renaissance and the Enlightenment were factors in the development of social welfare (Payne, 2005). These developments reduced the influence of the churches, and in their place grew municipal and organised charitable provision, although religious impulses and the desire for social prestige were still motivating factors for many of the philanthropists. Municipal and local charitable provision became increasingly interlinked with provision deriving from central government, as greater centralisation developed. The Elizabethan 1601 Poor Law had placed the responsibility for the care of those in need with the local parishes. The 1662 Act of Settlement empowered the parish overseer to remove from the parish any settler who could not give an assurance that they could find work within 40 days (Denney, 1998). While England's state provision at this time was local and variable, such provision was extensive in comparison with most other European countries (Payne, 2005). In France, provision for the poor was influenced less by charitable concerns than by fear of public disorder if such provision was not made (Fairchilds, 1976). Likewise, Gargett (1977) notes how social work in Zimbabwe (then Rhodesia) initially arose out of a need by the authorities to react to and control a troublesome population. Here we see links between social work, imperialism and colonial unrest. Such concerns were also influential in Britain, although it was the nineteenth century before they were explicitly expressed (Bailey and Brake, 1975).

The period from the mid-nineteenth century to the mid-twentieth century saw social work develop in the West, influenced by five interrelated factors: agriculture and then the manufacture of goods were industrialised; a middle class emerged to take local responsibility, and local government was municipalised in the nineteenth century; the power of the churches and religious belief declined and their welfare work was transformed into a more secularised form of caring; charity and women's welfare work became organised and, as social work developed, it became the site for a form of 'caring power'; and state responsibility for social intervention broadened, often because of a need to maintain social order in more complex and tumultuous societies (Payne, 2005).

The move towards the feminisation of social work is important here. Social relations for men were primarily seen as being through their work, for women through their domestic role. Where women were working outside the domestic sphere it tended to be encouraged through a caring, social welfare role. The common usage of the term 'nanny state' can be seen as reflecting this gendered view of social care.

Altruism or fear of the masses?

Political development around class is also important in understanding the origins of modern social work. Movements such as Chartism, which was concerned with obtaining the vote for working men, the rise of trade unionism and class conflict helped influence the development of social reform programmes. These influences helped create 'a tradition in Britain for general reform along collective and socialist lines that counterpoints, entwines and disputes with the development of social reforms and welfare in the latter part of the [twentieth] century' (Payne, 2005, p 24).

As people came increasingly to live in cities and towns, away from the tight-knit rural communities of the past, there was concern over issues such as moral breakdown, crime and health. Such sentiments were not confined to those we may consider to have been right-wing reactionaries: many intellectuals and popular writers, including George Bernard Shaw, Aldous Huxley, George Orwell and H.G. Wells, betrayed a fear of the masses, who were viewed as semi-human swarms liable to contaminate the nation (Carey, 1992).

The health of the poor became an issue of concern for the ruling and intellectual classes for a number of reasons. The demands of trade unions for improved conditions not only in work, housing and education but also in health coincided with the ruling classes' fear of military expansion abroad. To combat this external threat a healthy military force at home was necessary, a need undermined by the effects of poverty and malnutrition within the urban poor. Indeed the medical examinations for recruitment into the army before and during the First World War highlighted the appalling state of the nation's health. As the Association of Directors of Social Services note, 'social welfare legislation might not have been born as a gift to the people, but as a partial recognition of economic and defence necessity' (ADSS, 1982, p 3). In this instance the ruling and working classes shared a mutual interest in raising the health of the poor, although it was the bourgeoisie who set the pace of change (Bailey and Brake, 1975). Unease at the prospect of internal unrest, coupled with the fear of losing imperial power abroad, provided much impetus for social reform and a concern with the health of the proletariat.

Charity and philanthropy

There was a view that social development and its more adverse consequences generated many of the problems facing society, although there was also the view that the masses lacked proper morals or values because of deficient guidance or poor breeding. Improvements in working conditions, campaigns for voting rights and universal welfare systems indicated that capitalist development was generating inequalities and that ameliorating measures were necessary. The means of achieving this varied, for example the emerging Labour Party emphasised the role of the working class, while the Liberals strived to achieve social reform without it taking on an overt working-class allegiance.

The fear of working-class riots influenced the setting up of many of the charitable organisations of the day. The Charity Organisation Society (COS), established in 1869, was part of the movement whereby the middle classes would attempt to inculcate their values in the working class. Their task was to reward the deserving and control the undeserving poor. Altruism was mixed with trepidation, for example Samuel Smiles, writing in 1885, warned that 'the proletariat may strangle us, unless we teach it the same virtues which have elevated other classes' (quoted in Bailey and Brake, 1975, p 5).

The charity organisations were also the first to implement formal training for social workers. For Powell (2001, p 37), this training was an attempt to adopt the scientific 'method of observation and experiment, reasoning and verification, to the task of relieving the poor'. In 1903 the School of Sociology in London was established by the COS, nine years later it was incorporated into the London School of Economics. Lorenz (1994, p 47) describes this amalgamation as representing a 'historic compromise' with Fabianism. The rationale for the training of social workers under the new philanthropy was an attempt to instil some guiding principles into what was a chaotic growth of projects without much coordination. However, the tension between teaching macro societal issues to explain poverty, homelessness, child neglect and unemployment, and the need for social workers to work on an individual and cost-effective basis compromised this philanthropic ideal. As Lorenz puts it, 'With this step towards training, the philanthropic ideal necessarily transcends the boundaries of charity and enters the realm of social policy' (1994, p 47). Here we see the first formal links between social work training and the state, a relationship that has become increasingly complex and at times disharmonious and which we will look at in more detail later.

The COS established local offices in each Poor Law division, and – in an early attempt at joined-up working – a charity agent would work in liaison with the local Poor Law officer and local clergy. This agent would record the details of all those receiving charitable relief, and scrutinise applications for help from those outside the reach of existing agencies and in the last resort offer assistance subject to the agreement of the local committee. This led to the local COS office being the 'recognised centre of charitable organisation in the locality', and by 1872 under this approach the COS had 36 local offices (Powell, 2001, p 33). In 1890 a number of guiding principles concerning the administration of relief were published, titled *Charity organisation and relief: A paper of suggestions for charity organisation societies*. Some of these principles were that:

> each case must be treated individually, the welfare of the entire family must be considered; full enquiry must be made as to the causes of distress, needs, resources and character. Temporary help was to be given only if it was likely to produce permanent benefit, not merely because the applicants were honest and 'deserving'. Thrift was to be encouraged and repayment of help required, if possible. The assistance of kinship and neighbourhood networks was to be elicited and promoted. (Powell, 2001, p 34)

The tension between giving help without creating dependence, distinguishing between the 'deserving' and 'undeserving', assessing financial ability and familial and social networks has been, in one guise or another, a continual factor in social work and welfare to the present day. New Labour's 'hand up not a hand out', the 'underclass' debate (Lister, 1996) and the financial assessments completed during a Community Care Act assessment echo the concerns of the COS over a century ago.

The COS was heavily influenced by the principles of social Darwinism. Its charitable role as it saw it was to help those who needed assistance with interim measures that would enable people to be able to stand on their own two feet. Those 'undeserving' cases or those unable to survive would be left to perish, or be picked up under Poor Law provision. In 1871 one-third of applicants to the COS for assistance were refused. Such a position made the rapidly growing labour movement increasingly hostile to the COS, and began to cause internal rifts within the organisation, with some people opposed to the existing position. This was a clash between 'positivism and humanism, between those who advocated science and those who promoted social reform as an appropriate response to poverty' (Powell, 2001, p 34).

This clash led to a certain change of focus within the COS. While individual casework remained, there was an acknowledgement that there had to be some level of social reform that would produce less hardship for the individual. With this new focus the COS extended its work from housing to include other social issues such as sanitation, immigration and 'handicap'. Summarising nineteenth-century social work as espoused by the COS hierarchy, Powell notes that it was:

> a complement to the New English Poor Law of 1834 with its concept of 'least eligibility' formulated by the classical economists which denied the existence of poverty and admitted only to the problem of pauperism. The COS did not share this pessimistic view of a homogenous dependent class. They believed that many could ultimately share in the prosperity of industrialisation with a modicum of charitable assistance to the 'deserving' able-bodied poor temporarily in need. By implication the 'undeserving' poor should be left to 'their just desserts' and the disabled looked after by their own families, obviating the need for statutory provision. Natural law would take care of the rest, in keeping with the Darwinist thinking of the times. (Powell, 2001, p 35)

This view was expressed by Octavia Hill in 1901 at the Annual Conference of Charity Organisations:

> I wish I could convey to those who are here any of the deep conviction I feel that the working man and woman of our day is not the poor, helpless, dependent creature our stupid

doles or wide socialistic theories assume. He has thought, resource, power, capacity for commanding fair wages and common sense to expend them, if we would only let him alone to try. (quoted in Powell, 2001, p 35)

Inherent in Hill's pronouncement was a belief in the human subject as an agent of change. The profound effects of social deprivation were not ignored but there was a conviction that even the most damaged and destitute had the ability to improve their situation. The flipside to this individualistic approach, however, was that those who failed to improve their situation, especially after receiving the benevolence of the COS, were likely to be labelled as undeserving of further help, and their failure to exercise agency seen as due to individual pathology. Nevertheless, the passionate belief of people like Hill that saw people as shapers of their destiny is at times inspiring to read:

> By knowledge of character more is meant than whether a man is a drunkard or a woman dishonest: it means the knowledge of the passions, hopes and history of people, where the temptation will touch them, what is the little scheme they have made of their lives, or would make, if they had the encouragement; what training long past phases of their lives may have afforded; how to move, touch, teach them. (quoted in Butrym, 1976, p 2)

The individualistic approach of the COS may have had an optimistic view of the individual but it had a naive view of the role of the social in human behaviour. Out of these tensions emerged a new form of philanthropy that viewed poverty as more of a social problem than one of individual failing, as due to contradiction rather than evolution. The Guild of Help was an organisation that epitomised the new philanthropy. Rather than seeing a chasm between the charitable and the needy, the guild emphasised a more humanistic approach. As one guild newsletter put it, 'the Guild worker does not go in as a visitor from another world but as a fellow creature to be helpful' (quoted in Laybourn, 1995, p 155). This approach, while more humane than the preceding social Darwinist approach of the COS, nevertheless still encountered hostility from socialists, not only for failing to eradicate poverty but also because it had no hope of doing so, being dismissed as 'Gilded Help' (Powell, 2001, p 36).

The schools of the new humanitarian philanthropy approach to social work did not remain independent for long, their relationship with Fabianism taking them into an unequal relationship with the state. Lorenz discusses the British, German and Dutch schools and notes that 'Most of the schools founded on its [humanitarian philanthropic] principles came under direct state control in line with the state's unequally phased acceptance of their public welfare responsibility' (1994, p 47).

The 'settlement movement' was another factor in the early development of social work. The first settlement in Britain was established in the East End of London in 1884, with many more following both within and outside the capital. Taking a more sceptical approach to the COS's positivist belief in the inevitability of progress, the settlement movement favoured an appeal to humanitarian principles. It shared with the COS the idea that the better educated in society needed to reach out to the needy, encouraging its members to live among the poor in order to educate them and set them an example of how to live life. Accepting the social causation of many social problems the settlement movement attempted to raise the consciousness of the poor, which was at least an attempt to politicise the people of the communities in which they lived. Powell (2001) sees the main differences between the COS and the settlement movement as being ideological and also in class membership. While the COS represented the propertied upper class, the settlement movement (who mostly had disdain for the 'lower orders') was born of the social commitment of middle-class intellectuals. The COS had a positivist, optimistic belief in societal progress, while the settlement movement was dismissive of this naivety, instead appealing to 'humanity and reason: public knowledge of the social conditions of the poor coupled with political agitation would lead to an acceptance of the need for social change' (Powell, 2001, p 40).

Child welfare and protection issues were also important factors in the emergence of social work as a profession, The National Society for the Protection of Cruelty to Children, the National Children's Home and Dr Barnardo's Homes all being established and growing from the 1880s onwards.

These charitable organisations with their Christian and humanitarian principles adhered to the political consensus of 'less eligibility'. The workhouses were formally required to adopt harsh regimes in order to discourage people from entering them. Boards of guardians elected by ratepayers and a Poor Law Commission were established to control the workhouse system. As Jordan and Parton note, 'From 1834, till the 1930s, it was virtually unanimously agreed by national politicians that state services for the destitute – including orphaned children, the mentally and physically handicapped and the frail elderly – should be of a quality that was "less eligible" than the conditions of the poorest independent labourer' (1983, p 2). In essence this meant that the most vulnerable in society were prevented from having their individual needs met; the political consensus being that their quality of life had to be of lesser quality than that of the poorest worker.

Fabianism, welfarism and social work

Social work in this period grew rapidly, being seen by some as a social movement that rivalled that of politics and religion. It did, however, attempt to distinguish itself from both spheres:

> Social work was differentiated from politics in so far as it was less interested in the distribution of power than in the resolution of social conflict. Its goal was a social ideal, not a political system. As such, it was seen by its exponents as something better than purely political activity – in Barnett's words 'a sort of progress whose means would justify the end'. The differentiation of social work from religious movements was not always clear. In the Settlements, in particular, the social gospel was sometimes entangled with the religious gospel. The Charity Organisation Society solved this problem by seeing itself as an alternative to religious evangelism. Charity was the fruit of true religious faith. (Seed, 1973, pp 39–40)

This positioning of itself between two dominant spheres allowed social work to flourish. It could present itself as non-political while rationing services and differentiating between the deserving and 'undeserving' poor. By presenting itself as apolitical and therefore above political argument and conflict, it attempted to portray itself as a philanthropic enterprise. As separate from the Church, its moral stance could be presented from a humanistic perspective untainted by the decline in religious authority and tradition. Its main concern was not with the material circumstances of the poor but their character and morality (Jones, 1997).

By the late nineteenth to early twentieth century this philanthropic and individualistic moral view of poverty was becoming less sustainable. The COS stood accused of failing to alleviate poverty, with a series of surveys finding that up to one-third of the population of London and 28% of the inhabitants of York were living in poverty (Powell, 2001). Publications by socialists also highlighted the conditions of the working class in nineteenth-century England and were becoming more widely available (eg Engels, 2005 [1887]) and they exposed how out of touch the middle classes of the COS were with the reality of urban life in England at that time.

The disjuncture between the old apolitical stance of the COS, with its belief that individual moral failure was the root cause of people's problems, and the new approach of the Fabians was clearly put by one of the Fabian Society's founders, George Bernard Shaw. The Fabian agenda was to politicise the public and make them 'conscious of the evil condition of society under the present system' (quoted in Powell, 2001, p 45). For some commentators it was within this welfare state ideal that modern social work was firmly established, and it has continued to define itself in this context ever since. At a time when Marxist socialism was influential, the Fabians adopted a more gradual, evolutionary approach to social reform, taking their name from the Roman general Fabius Cuncator (the delayer), 'whose patience in avoiding pitched battles secured ultimate victory over the Carthaginian general Hannibal' (Powell, 2001, p 45).

Fabianism emphasised the need for social reform and saw the state as the main vehicle to achieve this. Social work, while having a similar humanist approach, was concerned with work with individuals who were beyond the auspices of the state. It was not concerned with structural change. With the moral pathology approach of the COS now seen as reactionary, social work was caught between the old and the new approach to alleviating human need. In the process of negotiating this juncture and trying to find a trajectory that it could call its own, social work began to embrace some of the emerging theories from psychology, most notably Freud's psychoanalytic theory. This has subsequently been seen as marking the 'triumph of the therapeutic' (Rieff, 1966).

The rise of the therapeutic

The early years of the twentieth century saw the gradual growth in influence of Freud's ideas regarding the individual psyche and of how the unconscious could explain individual problems. Social problems were not discounted as sources of conflict, but psychoanalytic theory sought 'treatment' in the context of individualisation and rehabilitation. However, it has been pointed out that the belief that social work practice was a homogeneous affair unremittingly adopting a purely psychoanalytic approach to their clients' problems is mistaken (Woodrofe, 1962). For example, Richmond's (1917; 1922) early attempts at theorising social work practice around this time, while attempting social diagnosis, were based on a sociological foundation. The 'sociological' social worker was looking for the cause of the individual's problem by the process of information gathering; such information would not only identify the problem (diagnosis) but, once it was identified, the belief was that the solution would become evident.

Johnson (1983) claims that psychological theories in the early twentieth century were insufficiently developed to account for human behaviour in anything but the most global, imprecise terms. According to Jordan (1984) it was the voluntary sector that embraced Freudian theory, with the public sector remaining largely resistant to its influence. For Powell (2001), Jordan's distinction between the public and voluntary sectors is correct. He argues that while Freud had a pervasive influence on the popular imagination, his views had little influence on public policy. His followers, who included social workers, may have seen him as imparting great insights but in general social work's pressing concern was with alleviating human suffering rather than with the interior character of human suffering. Others (eg Banks, 1995) acknowledge the influence of psychoanalytic theories derived from Freud but see derivatives of psychoanalysis as being more influential, for example, problem solving, psychosocial functioning and ego–psychological techniques.

Freudianism did, according to some (eg Jones, 1983; Powell, 2001), provide social work with a more humanistic and optimistic approach to the 'residium of poor', those that the Victorians and organisations such as the COS saw as beyond help and therefore needing to be left subject to the laws of social Darwinism. In the inter-war years, the belief that even the most damaged and socially inept could be improved by appropriate help and intervention began to influence social work practice. The belief that rehabilitative work was possible led to a move to discard older theories based on negative, repressive and Darwinist ideas and 'was critical to the possibility of social work's development as a major welfare strategy' (Jones, 1983, p 39). This belief became known as the 'rehabilitative ideal' and was enormously significant. For past social reformers, 'the very idea that the residuum had emotions or feelings worthy of respect and consideration was anathema to many past social reformers. Similarly, the idea that they could be restored to active citizenship through a caring strategy of casework and re-education would have been considered outrageous' (Jones, 1983, p 39). It should be noted, however, that such changes were not imposed by an altruistic government on a passive audience; the role played by the working class in pushing through social reforms and more liberal and extensive welfare systems was crucial to the process.

The ambivalence towards psychological theories in social policy and social work began to change towards a more accepting stance as the twentieth century passed. By the 1930s there was a considerable rise in the use of psychoanalytic theories. Although again the extent is often exaggerated, there was a decrease in emphasis on the social towards a more individualistic account of human behaviour and experience. As society turned inward so too did social work; the focus changing from the social situation to individual experience and in particular on early childhood experience.

As the 1930s progressed such a viewpoint became increasingly popular and could now be more accurately termed a 'psychiatric deluge'. This deluge did not only influence practice, it also influenced social policy enormously in the 1940s and 1950s (Woodrofe, 1962). In the US, Hamilton's work (1940; 1951), heavily based on psychoanalytic theory, was highly influential. Meanwhile in Britain psychoanalytic theory also became more popular within social work, especially in those areas concerned with mental welfare.

Influenced by both Freudian and then distinctively Kleinian schools of thought, psychoanalytic theory began to occupy an important place in psychiatric social work education, leading to a discussion as to whether such employees were primarily social workers or therapists (Irvine, 1978). It has been suggested that an articulate minority who viewed themselves as therapists had an undue influence on the perceived usefulness of psychoanalytic techniques in both education and practice. For example, Bree's (1970) research found that from its inception in 1947 to 1960, only 16% of psychiatric social workers had contributed to the *British Journal of Psychiatric Social Work*, many only once, suggesting that there was a silent majority of workers using a more intuitive and spontaneous practice that they were either unable or unwilling to articulate.

In 1969 the Association of Psychiatric Social Workers published a list that showed it had 1,350 associates, although many of these were retired, working abroad or had withdrawn from the profession for personal reasons. In England and Wales, 334 psychiatric social workers were employed in child and adolescent psychiatry, 189 in psychiatric hospital departments. Only 12 were employed in clinics providing out-patient treatment for adults only (Irvine, 1978).

At that time 59 were employed in or made a contribution to social work training (Irvine, 1978), which possibly supports Yelloly's (1987) claim that a form of quasi-Freudian psychology became the dominating paradigm of social work training. This training emphasised the psychological at the expense of the political, economic or material.

As Jordan and Parton put it, 'social workers were trained out of any political understanding of their work' (1983, p 3).

The social democratic truce represented by the setting up of the welfare state, being seen as highly progressive and of evidence that the market and social justice could coexist, led to a depoliticisation of poverty and inequality and helped pave the way for the rise of psychological explanations for human difficulty. This emphasised the need for diagnosis and treatment of the individual. Halmos (1965) demonstrates how this trend to set up state services that included social workers was incorporated by other countries in Western and to a lesser extent Eastern Europe. The outcome was similar to that in Britain, with political controversy being marginalised by a combined emphasis on technical and therapeutic training for social work staff.

The ascendancy of a therapeutic culture in Britain was relatively uncontested during this period (Furedi, 2004). One exception was Wooton (1959), who was vociferous in her criticism of the influence of psychoanalysis and other therapeutic beliefs into social work practice. For her, 'modern definitions of "social casework", if taken at face value, involve claims to powers which verge upon omniscience and omnipotence' (Wooton, 1959, p 271).

Wooton favoured more practical intervention, suggesting that social workers took confidence in their own particular skills rather than posing as para-therapists:

> The range of needs for which public or voluntary services now provide, and the complexity of the relevant rules and regulations have now become so great, that the social worker who has mastered these intricacies and is prepared to place this knowledge at the disposal of the public, and when necessary to initiate appropriate action, has no need to pose as a miniature psychoanalyst or psychiatrist: her professional standing is secured by the value of her own contribution. (Wooton, 1959, p 296)

In attempting to explain the rise of psychological and sociological theories within social work, Wilkes (1981) sees social work's desire to become a profession with a knowledge and theoretical base as leading to the embrace of both psychological and sociological explanations for human behaviour, both of which were emerging subjects rapidly gaining in popularity. This independent body of knowledge was necessary in order that the qualified social worker could be set apart (and above) from the unenlightened who did not possess such expertise.

It is important to note that within social work practice, while psychoanalytic theory was influential, in most cases it was a derivation from pure psychoanalytic theory into a hybrid that included other more social solutions to clients' problems. For example, Hamilton's (1940) influential text, while heavily based on psychoanalytic theory also acknowledged the need for the worker to take into account social resources in conjunction with counselling or other therapeutic approaches.

Summarising social work developments in the US during the 1930–45 period, Johnson (1983) identifies three main trends. The psychoanalytic approach already discussed was dominant but there was a challenge from those, such as Taft (1944) and Aptekar (1941), who favoured the functional approach. This approach saw the client–worker relationship as more of a partnership, as a search for common ground between them. As the relationship grew, the ability for change would also develop. During the same period there was also a rise in social group work and community work. It is important to note that these ideas were not embraced wholeheartedly, being modified and adapted in a spirit of eclecticism rather than adherence to any one school.

Of course, it was not the case that social conditions were ignored by the profession. Highlighting the work of the British Federation of Social Workers, set up in 1935, Lees (1972) cites examples of their concern with issues of social policy that affected their clients, for example around 'hours of work for boys and girls', and 'the homeless poor' and 'new housing estates and their social problems'. In 1950 the federation published an ethical code that emphasised the social aspect of such issues. Among others, the code required of social workers:

1. To help the public as members of a democratic community to take their full share in the social services, and to keep them informed on social needs.
2. To try to stimulate interest in, and supply information on, social questions, and influence social policy.
3. They should particularly encourage public participation, by enlisting the help of volunteers. (Lees, 1972, p 5)

While Lees is correct that there remained 'a concern for social reform and its achievement through political processes' (1972, p 2), his examples are evidence of this in certain limited settings only, and cannot be said to be indicative of the wider profession or the day-to-day work they undertook. Indeed, Freudian-based concepts soon expanded from the psychiatric services into mainstream social casework (Halmos, 1965).

While these approaches were only in their infancy, they are important to the argument of this book for two reasons. First, as will be shown later their influence is still substantial in current social work theory and practice. Second, it highlights the dialectical process by which material reality affects intellectual thinking and vice versa. For example, it is important to note that the ideas discussed earlier did not happen in a vacuum. They were approaches to the study of social problems and human behaviour that were influenced by other factors:

> The rich development of theory during the late 1930s and early 1940s was at least partly a result of the tremendous impact of the depression era on social work. No longer did older theories about personal deficiencies as the cause of poverty and deviance hold up. Rather, the influence of a person's situation was seen as how it affected his well-being. Psychological knowledge, particularly that based on Freud's work, provided understandings of deviance that looked at cause for deviance in the intrapsychic part of the personality and provided a usable, organized theory for assessing the personality. (Johnson, 1983, p 24)

Similarly, from the 1950s there was disillusionment with wider political change that also influenced the move to Freudian approaches to alleviating social problems. The main concern lay ultimately with the individual, but rather than being seen as due to a moral or Darwinian deficiency, some internal conflict, repressed emotional state or unconscious process was implicated. The social (with a very small 's') situation in terms of family and community process was a factor acknowledged as having a bearing on the individual psyche.

If the 1950s and 1960s are seen as the period when psychoanalytical techniques were particularly influential within social work, some writers noted a reaction against them in the 1970s and 1980s. Pearson et al (1988) suggest a number of reasons for this. First, analytically inspired 'social workers as therapists' were viewed as remote from the busy pressurised environment of the contemporary social work office. Second, an increase in legislation both directed and constrained what social workers could do in their attempts to cope with the casualties of a political and social context in which the role of therapy seemed peripheral; and third, psychoanalysis was viewed by the 'radical social work' movement as representing the 'case con' in which therapy was charged with deflecting attention from clients' material needs, although as Pearson et al note, 'one of the ironies of this "radical" rejection of psychoanalysis within social work [was] that it coincided with a renewal of interest in psychoanalysis' (1988, p 5). As psychoanalysis fell out of favour with social work it began to be embraced 'within the broader "New Left" and "counter-cultural" movements which were to be counted as an important part of the inspirations for social work's own "radicalism"' (Pearson et al, 1988, p 5).

This contradiction is an important one, for the radical rhetoric hid how it had been influenced and looked for support from those who subscribed to the therapeutic ethos. As a more class-based movement receded from influence there was a renewed embracing of the therapeutic. How this interaction has developed will be discussed in later chapters.

Defining social work

Attempts at defining social work have led to various interpretations of the social worker's role. It is worth considering some early definitions and some later ones to illustrate the changes. More contemporary definitions will be discussed in Chapter Four. Payne distinguishes between social work, 'as an *activity*, something that human beings do, and as a *profession*, a particular kind of occupational group' (1996, p 3, emphasis in original). This distinction allows us to differentiate between the familial or community type of caring help we all engage in and the type carried out by state or quasi-state organisations, although it is worth noting that while social work identifies itself as a profession this self-definition is not without some problems. Greenwood's (1957) five attributes that all professions possess are: systematic theory, authority, community sanction, ethical codes and culture. However, as Johnson (1983) notes, social work does not meet these criteria as readily as more traditional professions such as law or medicine, for example:

1. The profession generally agrees there is a core, or base, of knowledge that is used by the total profession. However, while there is a certain general agreement about the core, or base, consensus about the specifics of this base has not been reached.
2. The use of the term social worker to identify many persons who are employed by social service agencies but do not have a professional degree makes it very difficult for the general public to identify the contribution of professional social work.

3. Unlike other professions, social workers are usually employed by an agency or institution; thus, practice lacks a certain degree of professional autonomy accorded to professions like medicine or law.
4. Social work developed from a number of specialities and responses to human need. The melding of these various endeavours into one professional body is still somewhat incomplete. (Johnson, 1983, p 19)

It is clear therefore that any attempts at defining social work will be partial and open to dispute. They will also vary historically. In an early attempt to define social work, Reynolds, writing in 1935, saw it as concerning itself with:

> human beings where there is anything that hinders or thwarts their growth, their expanding consciousness, their increasing co-operation. Social case work is that form of social work which assists the individual while he struggles to relate himself to his family, his natural groups, his community ... we shall use no methods that in themselves hamper the growth of the human spirit. (quoted in Payne, 2006, p 35)

Reynolds' definition, concerned as it is with anything that thwarts human consciousness and growth, has no conception of societal norms or structures as being problematic or a focus of social work's concern. However, other writers of the time were making the connection and were defining social work accordingly. For Lurie, social work is about 'helping individuals to obtain relief, to register for and obtain employment ... to obtain health, educational and recreational services on some decent level ...' (1935, p 617).

Here we see an acknowledgement of the role of societal structures in the need for social welfare, with the capitalist economic crisis of the Depression era implicated in the lack of resources available to the community. These early and opposing definitions indicate that the social work role has always been a matter of dispute, and also that existing social relations were implicated in the cause of individuals' problems long before the radical social work movement gained prominence in the 1970s.

Definitions of social work also drew on Enlightenment philosophical traditions of universalism and a belief in social progress:

> Social work rests ultimately on certain assumptions ...
> without which its methods and goals can have no meaning.
> The axioms are, for example: human betterment is the goal
> of any society ... the general standard of living should be
> progressively improved; education for physical and mental
> health and welfare should be widely promoted; the social
> bond between man and man should lead to the realisation
> of the age-old dream of universal brotherhood. (Hamilton,
> 1951, p 3, quoted in Payne, 2006, p 36)

This appeal to universalism would, in the contemporary period, be seen as problematic at best, or more likely be seen as racist and discriminatory within social work discourse. The reasons for this change are linked to wider social theory and its influence on social work, which are discussed in Chapter Two.

By the early 1970s the interaction between the individual and society was beyond dispute, although there was disagreement on the weight each category warranted, with some still seeing the client as a case for treatment:

> The major system to which diagnosis and treatment are
> addressed is the person-in-situation gestalt or configuration.
> That is to say, to be understood, the person to be helped
> – or treated, if you prefer – must be seen in the context of
> his interactions or transactions with the external world; and
> the segment of the external world with which he is in close
> interaction must be understood. (Hollis, 1970, pp 35–6)

The same year, Younghusband gave the following definition, which is instructive in its appeal to a gendered rationality, a concept that was to be brought into question by later postmodern theorists: 'the ultimate aim of social work would be to promote the dignity and worth of the individual human person and thus to further the growth of man from within himself. This includes a constant obligation to be on the side of *rationality against irrationality and prejudice* ...' (Younghusband, 1970, p 9, emphasis added). As we will see, within a few years rationality, like universalism, rather than being seen as a weapon against irrationality and prejudice, would on the contrary be implicated as upholding and justifying oppression.

The National Association of Social Workers (NASW) in the US further attempted to define the work of social workers in 1973. According to them:

Social work is the professional activity of helping individuals, groups, or communities enhance or restore their capacity for social functioning and creating societal conditions favourable to that goal. Social work practice consists in the professional application of social-work values, principles, and techniques to one or more of the following ends: helping people obtain tangible services; counselling and psychotherapy with individuals, families, and groups; helping communities or groups provide or improve social and health services; and participating in relevant legislative processes. The practice of social work requires knowledge of human development and behaviour; of social, economic, and cultural institutions; and of the interaction of these factors. (quoted in Payne, 2006, p 41)

Here we see a more overt view of social work as not merely recognising societal conditions as problematic but also of the social worker as an agent whose role is to create a more favourable social situation by working with both clients and social institutions. Such an acknowledgement came to dominate future definitions, with the social worker seen as someone whose role was not only to change the person but also to change the wider environment:

Social work is the purposeful and ethical application of personal skills in interpersonal relationships directed towards enhancing the personal and social functioning of an individual, family, group or neighbourhood, which necessarily involves using evidence obtained from practice to help create a social environment conducive to the well-being of all. (BASW, 1977, p 19)

Social work is a form of social intervention which encourages social institutions to respond to individual needs, enabling individuals to use their resources and in turn to contribute to them. It holds that the capacity and dignity of the individual are enhanced by participation in the life of the community. To achieve this end, it contributes to adjustments in the distributions of power and resources and attempts to help people, whether as individuals or groups, to have sufficient control over their lives to increase their opportunities for personal choice and self-realisation. (CCETSW, 1975, p 17)

Of particular interest to the contemporary reader will be the absence of race, gender or other social identities in these definitions. Likewise, today's social work student would be struck by the absence of terms such as 'discrimination' and 'oppression', which are ubiquitous within the present-day literature. The definitions outlined serve to illustrate thinking around the role of social work in the period leading up to the mid-1970s. How this changed in the wake of the radical social work movement and its offshoots from the mid- to late 1970s onwards is the subject of Chapter Two.

But what do social workers do?

It will be useful at this point to detail the day-to-day work in which the social worker in the period under discussion would be engaged, in order to emphasise the diversity of the role, and also to allow us to look at what, if any, changes have occurred in recent years. Davies' (1981) work will be used for two reasons. First, it is a detailed account of the variety of activities social workers in the 1960s and 1970s were engaged in; second, Davies' work has come under attack in more recent years for its adoption of an apolitical stance, so it is a useful reference to view the later changes discussed in the next chapter.

Davies identifies 12 main areas in which social work has a role, which, echoing post-war welfarism, takes us 'from the cradle to the grave'; indeed, as role 1 will show, the intervention precedes the cradle:

1. The social worker counsels pregnant women who apply to have an abortion. He may prepare a report which could influence the decision of the consultant gynaecologist.
2. The social worker has almost absolute power to facilitate or prevent the process of adoption. He selects adoptive parents, advises the natural mother, and allocates the child.
3. The social worker is expected by the community to play a key role in preventing child abuse. He has the power to recommend the removal of a child whom he believes to be at risk of being harmed.
4. In respect of families with mentally handicapped children, the social worker expects to play a significant part in helping the child make the transition from childhood to adulthood.

5. The social worker organises the community service programme for offenders, whereby men and women of all ages do useful work under supervision instead of going to prison or being otherwise punished for crimes committed.
6. In a hospital, the social worker might offer a counselling service to any patient recovering after an unsuccessful suicide attempt.
7. The social worker – perhaps in a voluntary agency, but also in local authorities – provides a long-term support service to families in severe straits. Sometimes the commitment extends over several years.
8. The social worker acts as an advocate in support of a client whose tenure of a council house may be in jeopardy.
9. The social worker helps a discharged prisoner find accommodation.
10. The social worker co-ordinates the range of services made available by the local authority to make life easier for a severely disabled person.
11. The social worker arranges for an old person to be given accommodation when the time comes that independence is no longer feasible.
12. The social worker is responsible for arranging and superintending a pauper's burial. (Davies, 1981, pp 4–8)

It is clear that the range of work in which social workers are involved is extensive, as is the power they wield over certain categories of people in many aspects of their lives. Davies sees the main social work role as being that of maintenance, to maintain and foster growth for the clients of social work, seeing little role for the wider political activity espoused by the radical social work movement. Nevertheless, as a 'snapshot' of the day-to-day work of a busy social worker his list of roles is instructive.

This chapter has looked at key developments within social work and of how writers and academics have attempted to explain them. Much of what has gone before does, of course, carry on in contemporary debates. However, I will begin to challenge these later interpretations, and in the process criticise many of those who claim to espouse a radical, anti-discriminatory viewpoint. Central to this will be the contention that social work did not create these debates. While they may have taken on a specific form within professional discourse, they also were reflections of wider social conflicts and theoretical attempts to explain social developments.

TWO

Politicising social work

Functional social work: early 1970s style

The 1970s saw increasing attempts to organise social work as a profession. In 1971 there was both the publication of the first issue of *Social Work Today*, a trade magazine for the profession, and the setting up of the British Association of Social Workers (BASW). The following year saw the inaugural edition of the *British Journal of Social Work* (*BJSW*) arguably still, in academic terms at least, the most prestigious of the many social work journals. The *BJSW* was linked with the newly formed BASW, a link that was expected to draw criticism from some quarters, according to the inaugural editorial. To assuage fears that the link with BASW would compromise the content of the journal, the editorial is at pains to assure the reader that the editor has been given complete freedom over content, although BASW did have control over some financial aspects related to the journal (editorial, *BJSW*, 1971). The setting up of BASW, combined with the establishment of social service departments as set out by the Seebohm Committee of 1968, marked a period of consolidation for social work, bringing together different specialisms and activities under one department, with the aim being to work towards preventive, family-based work and to combat the inefficiency said to be a result of social care being provided by different local authority departments (Payne, 2002).

Attempting to organise the profession was one thing; uniting it was another thing altogether. There was a polarity between those with a functionalist and those with a more conflict-based view of society and social work. A functionalist perspective would see social work as concerned with the majority of society, working with the 'anti-social' and 'socially sick' in order to make them 'less of a liability and more productive' to wider society, as opposed to the more conflict-based approaches in which social work is viewed as more concerned with the minority who are 'underprivileged, weak and handicapped' (Rankin, 1970, p 9).

For Rankin, to classify the undeserving poor 'as if they were not liabilities but deserved help' is wrong, not because he believes the poor themselves deserve help but because 'these so-called "feckless" and undeserving parents often have very deserving children and it is usually impossible to help or punish one without helping or punishing the other' (1970, p 20). In such a viewpoint social problems are due to the innate weaknesses of people, not the result of social conditions. The fathers of problem families are mostly social failures, unskilled inefficient labourers of low economic value, and as such are considered by the rest of society as the undeserving feckless poor:

> We believe, however, that they are what they are for two reasons; (a) they were *born* with a well-below-average potential of strengths and skills into an environment that has aggravated these inborn weaknesses; (b) a vertically structured competitive society has to have a bottom and they are the natural bottom rung of the ladder. (Rankin, 1970, p 20, emphasis added)

This more conservative/maintenance view of social work is echoed 11 years later by Davies (1981) who, although in more respectful language, sees social work as being concerned with the maintenance of society by providing provision for those who, for whatever reason are unable to provide for themselves:

> In so far as there are common elements in social work they are best described by the general notion of *maintenance*: society maintaining itself in a relatively stable state by making provision for and managing people in positions of severe weakness, stress or vulnerability; and society maintaining its own members by virtue of social work's commitment to humanist endeavour. (Davies, 1981, p 3, emphasis in original)

Davies' humanistic belief is laudable and all too rare in contemporary social policy and social work, where, as I will show later, a darker view of humanity is evident. Nevertheless, maintaining society, by implication also necessitates the acceptance of established norms and practices. Such a view contains within it implications for those who fall outside established social norms.

Homosexuality, at the time still deemed to be a mental disorder by many (it was not until 1974 that the American Psychiatric Association declassified it as such), fell within the maintenance view of social work. According to Graham (1971) the role of social workers in relation to those with 'maladaptive' sexual urges was to utilise behavioural therapy techniques in order to change such behaviour. The case of a cross-dressing married man is discussed. In order to 'cure' him of his homosexuality, a course of aversion therapy is begun, whereby he is dressed up in women's clothes and make-up, and then given electric shocks. There then follows a period of 'stimulus satiation' that entails him having to wear plastic pants for days on end. The therapy was unsuccessful 'possibly because of the long history of maladaptive behaviour' (Graham, 1971, p 199). In another case a married man who had homosexual fantasies was also given aversion therapy and encouraged to be more assertive and manly.

These cases are illustrative of not only the view of homosexuality at the time; the ideology of the nuclear family and gendered relations is also apparent: male equals manly behaviour, dress and rigid heterosexuality, with the woman's role apparently being defined by her willingness or reluctance to have sex with her husband. 'Despite intensive traditional casework his wife's lack of co-operation [she had stopped having sex with her husband] remained' (Graham, 1971, p 199). The belief that homosexuality is bad, while (married) heterosexuality is good is evident in one of Graham's 'most successful cases', where a young man 'predominantly homosexual in arousal and behaviour, possessed some heterosexual interest [and is now] a year out of treatment, *married, and has no homosexual urges*' (Graham, 1971, p 205, emphasis added).

The early 1970s editions of both the *British Journal of Social Work* and *Social Work Today* contain very little discussion of race or cultural issues. Where 'minority rights' is discussed, the minority it refers to is hospital social workers (Jansen, 1971). Also, disabled people tended to be viewed within a medical framework, with social workers failing to offer much in the way of material or emotional support (Hudson, 1971).

Considering the above examples from the vantage point of today it is clear that social work theory and practice was open to attack. The critics came from both within and outside the profession, with the early focus being a class-based one.

Radical social work

The 1960s, especially the latter part of the decade, saw a wave of social protest across the Western world. Campaigns against Western military intervention in the 'Third World', and critiques highlighting the racist and sexist nature of many societal institutions, such as the family, the police and the judiciary were voiced. Social work was not immune from such critical analysis, and many radicals from both within and outside the profession subjected it to fierce attack. This became known as the 'radical social work' movement and was the title of an edited book by Bailey and Brake (1975), which became required reading on social work courses of the time. The editors were concerned that:

> social work, both as a body of knowledge and as a sphere of activity, has developed its theory and practice from the social sciences. The influence in particular of psychology has led to an over emphasis on pathological and clinical orientations to the detriment of structural and political implications. (Bailey and Brake, 1975, p 1)

What critical debate there was, according to Bailey and Brake, was reformist rather than radical, leading to a situation where 'the political, social and ideological place of social work has never been satisfactorily discussed, nor has its possible exploitation as an agent of social control been taken seriously' (1975, p 1). To address this, a news-sheet, *Case Con*, was published between 1970 and 1975, proclaiming itself to be 'a revolutionary magazine for social workers'. Its manifesto stated:

> Case Con believes that the problems of our 'clients' are rooted in the society in which we live, not in supposed individual inadequacies. Until this society, based on private ownership, profit and the needs of a minority ruling class, is replaced by a workers' state, based on the interests of the vast majority of the population, the fundamental causes of social problems will remain. It is therefore our aim to join the struggle for this workers' state. (quoted in Bailey and Brake, 1975, p 147)

Class is the predominant social division in this analysis. Rather than being an independent arbiter of justice or basic provision, welfare is seen as an instrument that serves ruling-class interests. For example, the contradiction between the government's attack on 'welfare cheats' is contrasted with its relatively lenient concern with income tax evasion, even though the latter is more costly to the Exchequer (Levi et al, 2007). The withholding of benefits can also be seen as a strategy to force striking workers to return to work, as they would be unable to provide for themselves or dependent others. In this way welfare cannot be seen as an apolitical activity – on the contrary, 'welfare lies at the centre of the class struggle' (Bailey and Brake, 1975, p 3). Radical social work challenged the 'achievement' of the welfare state and exposed its flaws, developing both practically and theoretically (Corrigan and Leonard, 1978). Radical social workers and Marxist academics were producing critiques of the welfare state long before the 'New Right' attack of the 1980s and 1990s became prominent.

Social work was identified not only as a prop for capitalist inequality, but also as a potential route through which to instigate social change and raise the consciousness of the working class by use of a more community-oriented social work (Popplestone, 1971; Bryant, 1973). For Popplestone, the community social worker sees 'social disorganisation as a problem of the client (community) and sees change being brought about through a relationship between the practitioner and the troubled community' (1971, p 94). The setting up of, for example, residents' associations and playgroups in this reading represents a benign form of social work removed from the social control aspects of the work. The community social worker must go on an active search for clients by attaching herself to groups or existing institutions. Popplestone's favoured communities are the newer housing estates and the dumping estates. He sees traditional working-class estates as difficult to attach to as 'such people tend to be hostile to professionals, and have already developed their groups for mutual aid and support' (Popplestone, 1971, p 100).

This view is illustrated by Bryant's (1973) review of the 1972 miners' strike in Ayrshire, Scotland. Bryant notes how social workers were viewed with 'considerable suspicion and hostility from the miners on the local strike committee. The front line [social] workers found themselves being labelled as part of the "system" with which the miners were in conflict' (1973, p 161). While the social workers maintained contact with the miners, the relationship remained strained by a sense of distrust. In this struggle the social workers were seen as part of the state machinery. In analysing this, Bryant feels that it was the miners' collective strength and ability to define the terms of the strike that led to social workers being viewed with suspicion; 'External organisations were defined and evaluated within the context of the conflict with the government – they were either for or against the miners' (1973, p 169). Such a polarisation meant that there was little room for manoeuvre, or as Bryant puts it, no 'subtle distinction in position' (1973, p 169).

With the growth of social services departments and the politicisation of many within social work, trade unions also grew in size and importance. Social workers now had their own working-class struggle to get involved in, which came to a head during 1978. Growing anger around pay, local negotiation rights, out-of-hours 'standby' duty and regrading culminated in strike action by social work staff in August

1978. The dispute spread to include 14 departments and lasted officially until February 1979, although seven departments remained on strike until March and the last, Tower Hamlets, did not return to work until June 1979. The size and length of the strike does not mean that it was unanimously supported by the social work profession. The social work magazine *Social Work Today* at that time carried reports and articles for and against both strike action as well as the radicalisation of the profession. There was also discussion and disagreement about whether the British Association of Social Workers should remain a professional body only or should apply for trade union status.

If there was no political consensus within mainstream social work, neither did the radical social work movement represent a homogeneous group in terms of either strategy or theory. Langan and Lee (1989) highlight three different, but at times interconnected approaches to political activity within the radical social work movement. First, there was the 'revolutionary approach', which emphasised the social control aspect of the state, which by implication included themselves. Second, they list the 'reformist approach' to welfare, which campaigned for socialist change while defending the gains of welfarism. Third, there was the 'prefigurative strategy', heavily influenced by feminism and the notion that 'the personal is political'. These strategists 'favoured changes that prefigured the future and transformed present relationships of dependency ... by working both *in and against the state*' (Langan and Lee, 1989, p 14, emphasis in original).

A mixture of both Hegelian and Marxist thought is evident here in the conflict over the role of the state in the resolution of social problems. Hegel's Absolute Spirit, embodied by the state, could reconcile the contradictions within society. For Marx, on the contrary the state and its representations within civil society had to be transcended, as rather than resolve contradictions within society they upheld those distinctions in favour of the ruling class (Bensaid, 2002).

The radical social work movement's inspirations were at times so diverse as to be contradictory. The Marxist analysis of the role of the state and its emphasis on structure did not rest easily with the phenomenological, subjective view of the 'consumer' of social welfare advocated by consumerists. Feminist critiques of social welfare added another dimension to the debate, with an emphasis on pluralism, micro approaches to power and an attack on the 'gender blindness' of many traditional Marxists. Langan and Lee (1989) also acknowledge that the lack of optimism for social change led many radical social workers to adopt a 'realist' approach, which sees little scope for change in the here and now and has as its objective a defence of existing services.

Bailey and Brake were mindful of many of these issues, implicating social work training for being too pragmatic, legalistic and of teaching sociological liberalism. They berated training for having:

> no discussion of the creation of social reality by hegemony. No examination is made, for example of the ways in which men define the world of women, heterosexuals define the world of homosexuals, whites the world of blacks ... Social worker and client relations are never explored in terms of power. (Bailey and Brake, 1975, p 9)

At issue here was whose view of the world was considered as reflective of truth, and who and which groups had the power to define, and in the process objectify, certain groups of people. While the writers would have seen their critique as being one based on 'standpoint theory' via a social class prism, it also led to standpoint theory being adopted more widely and can also be interpreted as implying cultural relativism.

Standpoint theory

Manchester Metropolitan University's social work course handbook, *Learning through practice: Guidelines for students and practice teachers*, includes the following statement: '"The truths" as articulated by oppressed groups are a critical part of the knowledge base which informs social work teaching and practices. Such groups will be afforded support and developmental opportunities to articulate their truths and have them accepted as valid' (MMU, 2007, pp 37–8).

The statement can be read as being influenced by feminist standpoint theory as articulated and developed by writers such as Hartsock (1987; 1998) and Harding (1987; 1991), or alternatively as a postmodern position advocating the equal validity of competing truth claims by a variety of groups. That such a statement can appear in a practice handbook indicates that this is no mere theoretical position; on the contrary it indicates the contested nature of knowledge and of allowing oppressed people to define themselves as subjects rather than being objectified by the powerful. Implicit within it is the belief that there is no one Truth, no grand narrative with which to explain society or the human condition. Indeed, postmodernism has been defined as 'incredulity towards grand narratives' (Lyotard, 1989, p xxiv). Instead of one grand narrative, there is a plethora of mini-narratives. Any claim to Truth is not only viewed with incredulity but is charged with leading to the silence and subordination of oppressed groups. For example, the social model of disability is a challenge to the previously dominant medical discourse, which viewed disabled people as individual tragic cases in need of medical benevolence.

The main contention of standpoint theory is that those without societal power – the oppressed and marginalised – can provide a more accurate, and objective, account of the social world. More objective should not be misunderstood as equating with a universal truth. Hartsock sees it more as moving from the notion of 'truth' to that of 'certitude', by which she means that one has 'credible knowledge, knowledge that is "good enough" to act on' (1998, p 77). The intention here is to avoid falling into a relativist trap in which all knowledge is equally valid, while acknowledging that each knowledge claim can be improved on, or indeed discarded, at a later stage in the light of improvements and/or challenges to the prevailing knowledge. In similar vein, Harding (1991) favours the notion of 'strong objectivity', which she believes an oppressed group has more claim to than the 'weak objectivity' of society's dominant groups.

In essence, both Harding and Hartsock acknowledge that 'social reality' from the perspective of any social group is both situated and partial, but that those in subordinate or oppressed groups have a better grasp on society by virtue of their social position. The attempt by the oppressed to understand and explain their subordinate subject positions gives them greater insight into social relations than those who may merely want to justify and sustain the status quo. Feminist standpoint theory seeks to extend Marx's insight, in that just as his understanding of the world from the standpoint of the proletariat allowed him to get beneath bourgeois ideology and gain a better grasp of social relations, a feminist standpoint is better able to understand patriarchal institutions and ideologies.

It is clear, that following both Hegel and Marx there is an emphasis on struggle to gain not only recognition but also liberation. This feminist standpoint sees itself as part of a historic process towards liberation. Echoing the Marxist notion of the working class seeking to end class society, including by implication their own class identity, Hartsock asks what she considers to be the fundamental question: 'How does this strategy [for change] contain at least the seeds of its own supersession?' (1998, p 70).

Feminist theorists, from this perspective, rather than merely describe a situation, attempt to question why it is the way it is. For example, instead of merely describing the percentage of women over men in low-paid, insecure employment, or indeed unpaid 'domestic' work, they would ask and seek to answer why it is the case that such situations have arisen, and are reproduced and accepted by many in society. Here, we can see how 'strong objectivity', with its emphasis on social constructionism, patriarchy and/or capitalist development, would give a better understanding of reality than the 'weak objectivity' of those defenders of the status quo, whose epistemological justifications may stress tradition, biology or religious doctrine. The emphasis is on understanding in order to instigate change, the intention being to make a difference in people's lives (Stanley and Wise, 1993).

Criticisms of standpoint theory include that it could lead to a focus on personal emotional beliefs that cannot be public or collectively reasoned about, that every explanation has to be further explained ad infinitum, and also that only personal issues are worthy of consideration. However, these objections can then lead to a 'refusal of reflexivity' that can leave us with 'a pretence to objectivity that will only work if there is a leap of faith, a subjective leap into a peculiarly dogmatic position' (Parker, 2005 p 33). The point Parker is making is that to accuse the feminist standpoint theorist of only wishing to talk about 'personal' issues necessitates a fixed, ahistorical account of what constitutes the personal sphere. The critic may have a point about a focus on the personal, but needs to be aware that what constitutes the personal and political spheres cannot be rigidly defined through time and space.

It is also the case that in her early work from the 1970s, reproduced in 1998, Hartsock details her own and others' awareness of the dangers of the 'personal is political' slogan being wrongly viewed as merely a form of identity politics. Individual subjectivity did not necessarily equate with a standpoint subject position. As Weeks puts it, transforming subject positions into standpoint positions involves 'an active intervention, a conscious and concerted effort to reinterpret and restructure our lives … *A standpoint is a project, not an inheritance*; it is achieved, not given' (quoted in Hartsock, 1998, p 80, emphasis added).

Feminist standpoint theory, by implication, also lends itself to any other oppressed group, whose subjugated position is seen as allowing them greater clarity than those outside the group. On the surface it appears to offer the potential for various groups to challenge existing ideologies. This emphasis on social change and a belief that there were social movements equipped to carry out the task appear to lie at the heart of standpoint theory. However, whether this is the case today, or indeed whether feminist standpoint theory developed at a time when such optimism had already receded is open to debate.

From macro to micro

This more critical analysis of power, questioning of dominant hegemonies and demand for recognition has proved influential. The earlier criticisms that social work training neglected an analysis of power or failed to consider cultural difference would be unfamiliar to anyone undertaking a social work course today; for example one university social work department's first point on its 'Anti-Discrimination Statement' is that 'This society is built on unequal power relations based on race, class and gender – a situation which is unjust. This has implications for peoples' lived experience of sexuality, age and disability. Such fundamental issues have to be addressed by this social work training programme' (MMU, 2007, pp 37–8).

Today, critics are more likely to claim that, rather than too little, too much emphasis is put on issues of difference and oppression (eg Phillips, 1994; Pinker, 1999). Whether Bailey and Brake (1975) would see today's emphasis on difference (around issues of race, gender, age, disability and sexuality) as wholly progressive is a matter for debate. Their main criticism was how hegemony created social reality, whereas the contemporary focus is away from such a meta-narrative approach to explaining reality, towards a more micro approach where social reality is constructed through discourse at the intersubjective level.

The radical social work movement can be credited for highlighting the political nature of social work, which at the time was predominantly a white middle-class occupation that was to a large extent aloof from the clients they dealt with. In this respect it represented a shift from the apolitical 'moral-ethical' and 'psycho-pathological' approaches that preceded it to one that explicitly highlights the political nature of the work. While radical social workers were never more than a minority within the profession, they had an influence far in excess of their number, 'in that they have prevented social workers from feeling too comfortable in a "professional" role, [and] they have reminded social workers of the importance of the analysis of power' (Ife, 1997, p 57).

Within this class-based critique there was a belief that the working class were agents of change, for some, of revolutionary change. To paraphrase Marx, their circumstances may not have been of their making but they had the capacity to change not only themselves but society as well. However, the radical social workers' main means of intervention was not through the world of working-class politics in the traditional sense of union meetings, political parties and industrial disputes. They saw their work activity as the main area of political activity. The working class may have been viewed as the revolutionary agents of change but they required professional state assistance to awaken their revolutionary consciousness.

Of significance here is the issue of seeing the workplace not only as a place of exploitation for the workers, but also as a way of engaging directly with the marginalised working class. The state was seen as problem and solution, as a way of raising working-class consciousness.

The approach by those of a Marxist persuasion was in one sense contradictory. While espousing a macro analysis of society, they were still operating at the micro level of personal change. This is not to be dismissive of micro-level work, making small but important gains for clients may not the revolution make, but for the individual in question it can make a significant difference to their standard of living. It did, however, reflect a wider sense of pessimism with change at the macro level. Langan and Lee (1989) noted the restricted potential for wider radical social change at the end of the 1980s and suggested that a micropolitical approach has considerable relevance for modern radical social work, while Pearson (1975) believed that a flexible, creative approach to progressive change was possible within departmental structures.

For Langan and Lee, the radical social work movement 'widened the scope of modern social work. It challenged the narrow preoccupation of traditional social work with the individual, introduced a wider set of issues and put politics on the agenda' (1989, p 2). They see the period from the mid–late 1970s to the late1980s as a period where changes in how social work operates necessitated a new approach for the radical project. They identify four factors influencing the new climate. First, there had been 15 years of economic recession from 1974 to 1989 that increased the numbers of people dependent on social welfare, which led to an increase in the workload of the average social worker. Second, high-profile inquiries into child abuse failings and a reaction against the 'permissive 1960s' personified by the liberal social worker led, at least in part, to a barrage of criticism of social workers, particularly radical social workers. Third, there was the increasing trend towards a more coercive, interventionist and policing role over those at the margins of society, especially 'deviant' families. And fourth, radical social work came under growing criticism from other groups, (for example black groups criticised the 'race blindness' of the early movement and highlighted the tokenistic and often ineffectual nature of equal opportunities and 'racial awareness training'). Likewise, other groups such as the disabled people's movement pointed out that their needs and interests had been ignored by the radical movement (Oliver, 1990).

Radical social work was also criticised because – among other things – in and of itself it has nothing to contribute to the reduction of wider interrelated problems such as unemployment and poverty (Rein, 1970). For Langan and Lee (1989), such criticisms are invalid as, while nobody believes social work by itself can solve such problems, to depoliticise the issues relegates social work to offering no more than 'band-aid solutions' to social problems. For them the key concept of the movement was, and still was at their time of writing, the 'empowerment of the consumer', with radical social workers urged to resist both 'new attempts by the authorities to promote the idea that poverty is a problem of individual failure' and 'the spread of reactionary ideologies and punitive measures' (Langan and Lee, 1989, pp 16 and 17), which at that time saw an increase in statutory child care powers at the expense of a more voluntary, participatory type of social work.

The development of an analysis of power away from a mainly class-based focus towards a more diverse discussion of how power and discrimination operates coalesced in the move for social work practice to be 'anti-discriminatory'. Langan and Day (1992) locate the impetus towards anti-discriminatory social work as coming from the encounter between feminist and anti-racist women in the 1980s. This framework was then developed to include other areas of discrimination, for example age and disability. Thompson (1993), author of *Anti-discriminatory practice*, believes that anti-discriminatory practice (ADP) shares with radical social work a strong critique of the power wielded by the state and statutory social workers. Where they differ, according to him, is that ADP is not as reliant on class analysis, giving equal if not more priority to issues of race, gender, sexuality, age and disability.

This emphasis on difference clashed with traditional social work, which had adopted an 'everybody is the same' approach. Racial difference was the first aspect of these less class-based approaches to come to prominence. There was increased recognition that Britain had a growing multiracial community, and that its members' experiences and worldview may be different from that of the majority white population because of the legacy of racism, cultural difference and issues of identity. It was acknowledged that everybody was not the same, and that an approach that treated everyone as alike was 'insufficient and we will be required to give more thought and consideration to the special needs and problems of the ethnic minorities' (ADSS, 1982, p 5). Here, people from minority ethnic groups are noted as different from the majority white population, not through biology or genetics but because of cultural variations and the experience of racism within British society. To address this, there was a move towards 'anti-racist', 'anti-discriminatory' and 'anti-oppressive' social work. Difference was to be recognised, acknowledged and respected.

Anti-racism and anti-oppression

According to the International Federation of Social Workers, 'the main aim of social work is to alleviate poverty, to liberate vulnerable and oppressed people with the ultimate aim to promote social inclusion', (quoted in Horner, 2003, p 98). This definition was also adopted in England by the now disbanded Training Organisation for the Personal Social Services (TOPSS) (Horner, 2003, p 98).

As we have seen, it was the politicisation of social work in the 1970s that highlighted the way social welfare and social work individualised social problems. Rather than being seen as due to the moral failings of the poor, poverty and marginalisation were seen as the results of wider political and structural inequalities. This early critique, focusing on social class, was itself in turn seen as problematic, being charged with ignoring or indeed perpetuating other forms of oppression such as racism or sexism. The 1980s and 1990s therefore saw the focus move to anti-racist and anti-oppressive practice within social work, with the agenda widening further to include issues such as disability, sexuality and age-related discrimination.

Such developments were the result of a number of factors. The 1980s saw much political unrest over social inequality and the impact of racism on the black community. Black activists, community groups and organisations highlighted the way in which their communities were discriminated against by the police and judicial system, education departments and housing policy and practice (Gilroy, 1987). This critique and resistance towards discriminatory welfare practices also applied itself to social service departments. Social work theory and practice was exposed as pathologising and controlling black people: for example, black people were more likely to have their children removed and placed in residential care (Bebbington and Miles, 1989), and more likely to be compulsorily admitted to hospital under the 1983 Mental Health Act than their white counterparts (Francis, 1991).

This increasing recognition of the unequal nature of British society was hugely influential within social work training in the mid- to late 1980s, culminating in the publication of the Central Council for Education and Training in Social Work's (CCETSW) second edition of *Rules and requirements for the Diploma in Social Work (Paper 30)* (CCETSW, 1989b), which emphasised the need for an anti-racist approach and the adoption of a policy that stated that:

> racism is endemic in the values, attitudes and structures of
> British society including that of social services and social
> work education. CCETSW recognises that the effects of
> racism on black people are incompatible with the values of
> social work and therefore seeks to combat racist practices in
> all areas of its responsibilities. (CCETSW, 1991, p 6)

While *Paper 30* (CCETSW, 1989b) uses the terms 'oppression' and
'discrimination', it does not detail what it understands the difference
between them to be. Nevertheless, it states that a competent social
worker shall demonstrate 'knowledge and understanding of' and
'develop an awareness of the interrelationship of the processes of
structural oppression' (CCETSW, 1989b, paras 2.1.4 and 3.1.4).
However, a later CCETSW publication, its first on gender issues, gives
the following differentiation: 'Anti-discriminatory practice will work
to a model of challenging unfairness. Anti-oppressive practice, however,
works with a model of empowerment and liberation and requires
a fundamental re-thinking of values, institutions and relationships'
(Phillipson, 1992, p 15).

In an indicator of the importance that was being placed on
terminology, Phillipson suggests that student awareness of gender
issues can be tested by way of monitoring whether they stop referring
to their wife/husband/girlfriend/boyfriend as such and start to talk
about their 'partner'. Social work education and practice required a
commitment to, and demonstration of, anti-racist and anti-oppressive
practice from students in order for them to gain professional status.
Students and practitioners are expected not only to have an awareness
of the construction and perpetuation of social divisions, but also
to demonstrate in practice how they have challenged the norms,
assumptions and behaviours that lead from them. In contrast to the
earlier definitions of social work, there was now an explicit political
agenda.

In one sense this was a remarkable achievement. The 1980s was a
period of Conservative political power with Margaret Thatcher the UK
prime minister. A key aspect of the Conservative Party's programme
was an attempt to create political hegemony around free market
economics and a return to 'traditional values' around the family and the
nation state. However, such Conservative rhetoric disguised a society
where conflict over politics and values was never far from the surface
(Penketh, 1998).

Riots in the predominantly black areas of Bristol (St Paul's),
Manchester (Moss Side), Liverpool (Toxteth) and London (Brixton

andTottenham) brought to the surface the underlying tension between black people and the police (Gilroy, 1987). Positive role models for black and Asian youth were conspicuous by their absence (Syal, 1994).

The Conservative Party's appeal to 'traditional values' merely exposed the lack of consensus as to just what such values were and who benefited from them. And, while the Labour Party was out of central government, it had control of many inner city boroughs through which it attempted to push through a 'reformist left' politics. The accommodation within the Labour Party of both black and women's groups was recognition that issues of gender and race could not be ignored, although such a process helped to institutionalise difference. Labour-controlled councils increasingly adopted 'equal opportunities' statements, which by their nature were an acknowledgement that inequality existed. Some such authorities, for example Hackney, pressed CCETSW to address the inadequacies of much social work training, which as it stood was ill preparing students to work in an anti-racist manner. According to Penketh (1998) CCETSW's anti-racist initiatives resulted from a combination of struggle by black social workers and students, rising acknowledgement of institutional racism within welfare agencies and an anti-Thatcherite political culture within many local authorities.

In order to be approved by CCETSW, social work training providers had to develop 'Clear and explicit anti-discrimination and anti-racist policies and explicit practices and procedures which provide evidence that these policies will be implemented and monitored in all aspects of the programme' (CCETSW, 1989a, p 22).

Penketh argues that the understanding of racism developed

> from individualistic explanations based on personal attitudes and behaviour, to a recognition that racism is a phenomenon that exists, and is structured within the practices of all British institutions, including social services departments, local authorities and higher education institutions. This reconceptualisation of racism highlights the manner in which individuals who may be genuinely opposed to racism can behave in ways which inadvertently discriminate against black people by following uncritically, the activities, 'norms' and unquestioned assumptions of the institutions within which they are located. (Penketh, 1998, p 37)

While there was this recognition, in practice local authorities still directed considerable effort to individualistic solutions to the problem of racism. For example, although the Greater London Council established London as an 'anti-racist zone' in 1982 and declared 1984 to be 'Anti-racist Year', its poster campaign still portrayed racism as a moral individual phenomenon. One poster asked 'Are you a racist? You'd be a much nicer person if you weren't.' Another read, 'If you are a racist you have a problem. Don't you have enough problems already?'. Apart from being criticised for being sanctimonious and individualistic, local authorities were also attacked for portraying the public as the problem and themselves as the solution, conveniently overlooking employment and housing policies that had historically marginalised the black population (Gilroy, 1987; Tompson, 1988).

As discussed earlier, the social work profession faced a similar attack. Its image as a benign provider of welfare had already been attacked along class lines, but its role in both the production and reproduction of racist ideology and practice was increasingly exposed. Dominelli (1988), in her book *Anti-racist social work*, was unequivocal about both the extent of the problem and the necessary steps required to overcome them. The first two chapters are entitled 'Racism permeates social work ideology and practice' and 'Social work training is imbued with racism', although her criticism was not of social work per se, just of current practice. With effort, she believed, the profession could atone for past sins by incorporating 'anti-racist' practice. It was noted that, since many social workers and students saw themselves as working within a caring profession and opposing social injustice, they found it difficult to come to terms with the possibility that they themselves might be perpetrating injustice through racist or sexist practices (Penketh, 1998).

As it developed, the term 'anti-racism', while still a discrete and specific term, in an acknowledgement of its egalitarian principles, and in an attempt to avoid the dilemma of creating a 'hierarchy of oppressions', embraced other areas of inequality, for example sexuality, disability and age, leading to a focus on 'anti-oppressive practice' (AOP) (eg Dominelli, 1996; Macey and Moxon, 1996). AOP has been defined as:

> A form of social work practice which addresses social divisions and structural inequalities in the work that is done with people whether they be users ('clients') or workers. AOP aims to provide more appropriate and sensitive services by responding to people's needs regardless of their social status. AOP embodies a person centred philosophy; an egalitarian value system concerned with reducing the deleterious effects of structural inequalities upon people's lives; a methodology focusing on both process and outcome; and a way of structuring relationships between individuals

that aims to empower users by reducing the negative effects of social hierarchies on their interaction and the work they do together. (Dominelli, 1996, pp 170–1)

The move to AOP has been both influenced and challenged by postmodernism and poststructuralism. Influences include a suspicion of grand narratives in favour of many competing narratives, power as operating at a variety of loci and the importance of language in constructing subjectivity (eg Parton, 1994). Challenge has come from postmodern writers (eg Fawcett et al, 2000) who argue that AOP's tendency towards 'oppositional discourses' (eg oppression/ emancipation; racism/anti-racism; masculinity/femininity) can in fact 'often extend the very relations of domination that they are resisting' (Fawcett and Featherstone, 2000, p 13).

However, they share the view of power as operating at a variety of levels, which means that the concept of oppression can be widened. For example, 'adultism' is held to mean the oppression of children by adults (Dalrymple and Burke, 1995). According to Doyle:

> child and 'elder' abuse and the mistreatment of dependent younger adults is at one end of the continuum of oppression with societal discrimination at the other … Oppression, whatever its form, has four essential components: the misuse of power, processes of objectification, the silence of witnesses and the entrapment or accommodation of witnesses. (Doyle, 1997, p 8)

'Oppression' is here characterised as being the exploitation of difference, in the way Preston-Shoot (1995) uses the term. This differs from Singh's (1996) focus on oppression as the 'denial' of difference. It would, after all, be foolish to deny that children are not different to adults. In these readings oppression is expanded from earlier notions where it meant the systematic denial of democratic rights to certain sections of society (for example, women and black people), to include interpersonal cases of abuse. It can also, as in the case of children, also confuse what can be a natural power imbalance, children *are* dependent, with a social differential.

This concern with 'minimising the power differences in society' (Dalrymple and Burke, 1995, p 3) is presented, not as a reaction to criticisms of anti-racist practice, but as a radical measure that moved 'from the narrow, exclusive focus on racial oppression to a broader, more inclusive understanding of the links between various forms and expressions of oppression' (Macey and Moxon, 1996, p 309). It also broadened the scope of social work intervention. If oppression was operating at every level of society, including intimate interpersonal relationships, then the anti-oppressive social worker had a licence to intervene, highlight and minimise such power imbalances.

This overt politicisation of social work did not go without a response, from both within and outside the profession. It provoked much debate, hostility, policy and personnel changes, and led, according to some, to a dilution of social work's commitment to an egalitarian society, in effect leading to a depoliticisation of social work. Such reactions are the subject of the following chapter.

THREE

'Depoliticising' social work

Introduction

The General Social Care Council (GSCC) set up under the 2000 Care Standards Act replaced the Central Council for Education and Training in Social Work (CCETSW) as the governing body of the social work profession. A search of its website (www.gscc.org.uk) in June 2007 with the keyword 'oppression' found a mere five results, only two of which are in policy documents (the other mentions were in two literature-based discussion documents, and one speaker biography). This hardly constitutes an obsession with the concept and appears to indicate that the new body has shed the more political outlook of its predecessor, lacking the overt, controversial anti-racist statement contained in CCETSW's *Paper 30* of 1989.

It is certainly the case that the more political stance of social work and concomitant move to endorse anti-racist and anti-oppressive practice (ARP/AOP) did provoke a reaction. For some it was an establishment-backed backlash against those concerned with the promotion of social justice (eg Dominelli, 2002; Mullender, 2003). Therefore, having sketched some of the influences on the move to AOP in the previous chapter, it is necessary here to look at some of the criticisms that it has attracted. The focus will be on three main areas: first that AOP was ideologically driven and was itself oppressive, second that it focused on 'trivial' issues of language and terminology and third that it was a top-down divisive approach that was detrimental to the struggle against racism. Finally, the AOP response to these issues and the concept of the 'backlash' are discussed.

Political correctness and the power of words

Social work's commitment to ARP/AOP was criticised for being ideologically driven by political zealots who would not accept deviations from the anti-racist doctrine, intimidating colleagues and students into a new conformity. According to Phillips, 'the anti-racism taught to trainee social workers has nothing to do with promoting freedom and equality; rather it explicitly rejects such principles' (1994, p 50). For Phillips, trainee social workers may have been encouraged to think, but their thoughts quickly had to get into line with the institutional hierarchy. They were free to think, so long as their thoughts concurred with the new establishment, which was the antithesis of freedom. The idea that racism is all pervading was also ridiculed. Certain institutions may have racist cultures and racial prejudice may be a general problem, but it does not follow that all institutions behave in such a prejudicial manner. Such a claim is, according to Phillips, little more than propaganda.

Other criticisms were that while the proponents of ARP/AOP insisted that all conduct must be anti-racist and anti-oppressive, it was, of course, left to them to decide what constituted not only racist or oppressive behaviour or language, but also what was the 'anti' in ARP/AOP (Pinker, 1999). As Webb put it:

> Judgement, censure, righteousness and watchfulness – all of which must perforce attend anti-sexism and anti-racism if they are to succeed – are also the defining attributes of the ideal-typical puritan. To the puritan falls the heavy obligation of practising extreme strictness in matters of morals and a developed sensitivity to breaches in the correct code of behaviour or thought. (quoted in Pierson, 1999, p 61)

To be accused of being 'politically correct' (PC) was not recognition of the legitimacy of your viewpoint, but on the contrary was meant in a derogatory fashion, used as a silencer to dismiss your views as being unworthy of serious consideration. It was also to be accused of wielding professional power in a moralising way against the poor. According to Dent, the 'PC police were swapping the pursed lips of "you should see the state of her kitchen" for the pursed rhetoric of "you should *see* her ideology"' (1999, p 28, emphasis in original).

One criticism of ARP/AOP that tended to personify charges of political correctness was that it paid too much attention to language, for example in censoring certain words for their inappropriateness and lecturing people on their choice of terminology, thereby implying that changing the vocabulary of the nation would ease social inequality. This approach was exemplified by tabloid press sensationalism, but a more serious, if still jocular critique comes from one commentator:

I used to think I was poor. Then they told me I wasn't poor I was needy. They told me it was self-defeating to think of myself as needy, I was deprived. They then told me deprived was a bad image, I was underprivileged. They told me underprivileged was over used, I was disadvantaged. I still haven't got a dime. But I sure have a great vocabulary. (quoted in Philpot, 1999, p 13)

The point Philpot is making in using the quote is that raised awareness does not equate with improved material resources. Dropping 'the Third World' in favour of 'the Developing World' does not improve the quality of life or alleviate the hunger of the people living in poverty. The poor have more to be concerned with than pedantic, linguistic protocols.

Such critics of the way in which social work was developing do provide an appropriate cautionary note. If social work and social welfare has historically been an instrument for oppression and re-enforcing either class, race or gender stereotypes, as proponents of ARP/AOP insist, then care has to be taken not to embrace the contemporary moral consensus uncritically.

While this is the case, the very hostile reaction to the 'obsession with words' for its trivial nature exposes the reality that it is not trivial at all. Cameron expresses her frustration at the self-contradiction inherent in those who get so inflamed about a 'trivial' issue, 'If the point is so trivial, I want to tell this person, "please humour me by conceding it. If it really doesn't matter what words we use, then let's just do it my way and both of us will be happy"' (1995, p 140). However, the reduction of the campaign for equality to arguments over linguistic niceties led to a focus on administrative, not material, measures to combat inequality.

Such measures increasingly took on an authoritarian edge as local authorities, including social workers, became concerned with enforcing 'appropriate' terminology. The theory and rhetoric may have acknowledged wider structural problems but practice could remain at the level of correcting language or behaviour. For example, in showing how they have met the requirement to act in an anti-oppressive way and to combat discrimination, the following quotes, which I have come across from students in their university practice placement reports, are not uncommon: 'I have tried to do this on a regular basis, as I have heard racist and sexist comments generally from the young people'; 'There was one incident where one boy used very racist comments'. Similarly, Collins et al quote one student's evidence; 'Anti racist practice in particular I put into action by challenging some residents' views and comments. I feel that I have learned to do this in quite a constructive way' (2000, p 38).

It would be a mistake to blame the students for such a situation. Much social work training emphasises the power of language, and they are merely encountering a major practical problem with AOP. In their working day they are unlikely to change the political system, but in an individual way the anti-oppressive social worker can use what power they do have to preach to the disadvantaged. This is not to dispute the power of language. Indeed, the very use of the term 'political correctness' is illustrative of both the power and importance of language. As Thompson notes, 'The fact that "political correctness" has become a term of ridicule illustrates the basic point – the power of language to reinforce existing power relations' (2002, p 94). The term can be utilised to justify the status quo, its very repetition enough to close off debate and absolve the speaker from having to defend their views or practices.

A concern with language within social welfare is important; the production, interpretation and reproduction of language are integral to social work:

> Its textual nature is demonstrated at every turn: the essays, process recordings, placement reports; the case records, applications, letters, case conference and court reports. From the process of applying to go on a training course, through the training programme itself, to the daily practice of 'professional' workers – social work is inescapably involved with the production and reception of text. (Turney, 1996, p 2)

Likewise, the role of discourse in identity formation, subjectivity and the construction of 'reality' in the form of 'truth claims' are important areas for consideration. As Humphries (1997) notes, discourses produce 'truths' and such 'truths' are necessary for the exercise of power. While too much emphasis on discourse can be problematic, for example from a Marxist perspective human action precedes discourse; the recognition of the importance of discourse in not only reflecting but producing and reproducing social reality is an appropriate area of social and political investigation. However, it is also the case that the relationship between signifier and signified is not constant, but subject to various social and political influences that necessitate a critical stance in order that changes in the meaning of concepts and terms can be identified (Parker, 2002). In other words, what is classed as 'anti-racist' or 'anti-oppressive' will change historically and its meaning will be debated at each juncture.

Social change from the top down

The role of social work academics and professionals in the implementation of AOP has also been criticised for being driven from above, for being a 'top-down' activity from a reformist political tradition of engineering social change that was not owned by rank and file social workers, but rather was imposed on them from on high (Penketh, 2000).

Penketh notes how CCETSW's policies contained a major contradiction:

> CCETSW is a state agency, social work is a practice within which the dialectic of 'care and control' is crucial. Paper 30 denounced the endemic nature of racism in Britain and its institutional and structural nature, suggesting it was embedded in dominant social relations, and hence could not be removed until those social relations had been radically transformed. However, this is a revolutionary solution to the problem, and social work is not a revolutionary activity … (Penketh, 2000, p 129)

She goes on to note that aspects of the job, for example probation, involve an element of controlling or 'soft policing' sections of the black community. Similar accusations can be made of mental health services (Skellington, 1996) and more recently in social work around immigration and asylum (Hayes and Humphries, 2004).

For Sivanandan, the incorporation of black sections within the Labour Party and local government, which influenced the trajectory of social work training, was not politically progressive as such people were 'no more representative of black working people than the Labour Party is for white. In fact, black politics has to cease to be political for blacks to get into politics' (1985, p 15). Sivanandan's point is not only that the creation of a new black middle class does not necessarily improve the lot of black people in general, but also that this entails an accommodation with existing capitalist social relations that necessitated a more micro analysis of social power. This led to local government, including social service departments, promoting or effecting an anti-racism that emphasised a psychological or affective approach to combating racism. While such moves are presented as extending democracy to groups that have hitherto been neglected by the political process, it encourages affiliation to be made on the basis of ethnic identity rather than political beliefs and shared vision.

The dangers of 'entryism', of trying to alter the system from within, were also highlighted. As Totton points out, 'while we are altering the system *it* is also altering *us*: working away at our sense of priorities, our language, our style' (1997, p 115, emphasis in original). In other words, there was a danger of ideals being corrupted, which for Jacoby became the reality:

> Once past the jabber about hegemony, difference and domination, this politics is defined by appointments and jobs, the not so revolutionary demand to be part of the university bureaucracy or the corporate world. In cruder terms, radical multiculturalists want more of their own people in the organization. This is fully understandable, but it is not radical, and it is barely political. It suggests patronage, not revolution ... Once upon a time revolutionaries tried, or pretended to try, to make a revolution; they harboured a vision of a different world or society. Now dubbed radical multiculturalists, they apply for bigger offices. (Jacoby, 1999, p 64)

He went on to note the more ideological problem facing the advocates of the politics of difference and identity. Devoid of ideas as to how the future could be shaped, pluralists embrace all ideas. Pluralism becomes multiculturalism, 'the opium of disillusioned intellectuals, the ideology of an era without an ideology' (Jacoby, 1999, p 33).

This move towards a celebration of cultural difference, of competing ethnicities and equally valid viewpoints, would lead to a dilution of the struggle against oppression. Whereas racism divided communities, it was argued that multiculturalism would further fragment them (eg Sivanandan, 1985; Malik, 1996). This is encapsulated in the endless 'etc' of difference, where an additional identity can be forever added: 'Black women are treated differently from white women, lesbians are treated differently from heterosexual women, disabled women are viewed differently from able-bodied women, older women are viewed differently from younger women' (Dalrymple and Burke, 1995, p 8). And, of course, black disabled women are treated differently from black able-bodied women and so on. Such observations may be useful in the realm of interpersonal relations, but are problematic in trying to develop a form of collective consciousness for wider political change.

The implication in this concept of 'otherness' is that differences are insurmountable, which can lead to a policy of cultural separation, for example in the debate over same-race adoption (Molyneux, 1993), where race is seen as the primary marker through which people are viewed.

Reconsidering the 'backlash' against ARP/AOP

Criticisms of ARP/AOP are likely to be dismissed as being part of a New Right backlash against progressive, egalitarian procedures that threaten the privileged power positions of a white, male–dominated society (eg Penketh, 2000; Dominelli, 2002). Dominelli (2002) argues that there was a media–orchestrated backlash against anti–racist social work. She claims that anti–oppressive social work was deemed a politically subversive operation that threatened the status quo and therefore was attacked by those opposed to social change, who questioned its relevance and effectiveness. Accusations of 'political correctness' were used to ridicule and silence those seeking change. For Mullender, it is 'the most damaging phrase in the English language [which] has been employed constantly, in a slick backlash reaction' against social work's mission to promote equality (2003, p xii). Others (eg Alibhai–Brown, 1993) liken the campaign against anti–racism to the anti–communist witch–hunts of post–war US. Those opposed to AOP are said to be fearful of change, a fear that is 'rooted in a loss of taken–for–granted privileges accorded to them through an inegalitarian social order' (Dominelli, 1998, p 11).

It is certainly the case that the tabloid press of the late 1980s and early 1990s delighted in ridiculing many of the policies and practices of left–wing councils, social work departments included. It is also the case that Virginia Bottomley, when Conservative secretary of state for health, accused social work of being preoccupied with 'isms' (racism, sexism, ageism, disablism, etc). Such criticisms did indeed have an effect on policy, with the appointment of Jeffrey Greenwood as chair of CCETSW in 1993. While declaring his commitment to equal opportunities, Greenwood also pledged to rid social work training of 'politically correct nonsense' (quoted in *The Independent*, 28 August 1993). This led to a revised *Paper 30* being published in 1995, with the explicit references to race and anti–racism dropped. The introduction of a 'competence–based' model of assessment for trainee social workers, plus the 'new managerialism' of the 1990s were also cited as being part of the reaction against AOP (Dominelli, 1996).

The move to a competence-based model of social work training was further criticised for being more suited to managers and the state than with overcoming the disadvantages faced by clients of social work. For Dominelli, 'competencies in social work are a set of highly technical, decontextualised practice skills which can be broken down into smaller and smaller constituent parts that can be carried out by personnel trained to a specified level' (1996, p 163). It represented the 'Taylorisation' of professional tasks and by separating and 'freezing' complex social dynamics the competence approach fragments 'the qualitative nature of social intercourse and abstract[s] it out of existence' (Dominelli, 1996, p 163). The competence-based approach also allowed employers and the state to exert control over workers, clients and service providers as they had to enter into contracts, the specifications of which had been drawn up by the state.

However, the move to a competence-based model of social work training was not a reaction to the 'radical' politicisation of social work; in reality the changes ran in tandem. CCETSW was implementing proposals for the assessment of competence at the same time as it was pronouncing on the extent of racism within British society.

The introduction of the new social work degree in 2003 could be seen as a further example of this move to cleanse social work of its more political stance. For example, in introducing the plans for the new degree, which saw the time spent on practice placement being increased from 130 to 200 days, Jacqui Smith, at the time the minister for health and who led the reform of social work education as part of the Modernising Social Services Agenda (DH, 1998b), commented that:

> Social work is a very practical job. It is about protecting people and changing their lives, not about being able to give a fluent and theoretical explanation of why they got into difficulties in the first place. New degree courses must ensure that theory and research directly informs and supports practice. The new degree will require social workers to demonstrate their practical application of skills and knowledge and their ability to solve problems and provide hope for people relying on social services for support. (Department of Health, press release, 22 May 2002)

The call is for more practical hands-on work, with the role of theory being merely to influence social work practice rather than to give insight into any wider structural or political issues, a point Smith emphasises in her foreword to the *Requirements for social work training* document (DH, 2002b). The same document also stipulates that social work training providers must 'ensure that the teaching of theoretical knowledge, skills and values is based on their application in practice' (DH, 2002b, p 3). Just in case we have not got the message it reminds us further on that, 'The new degree is all about *practice* and academic learning must support this' (DH, 2002b, p 8, emphasis in original). The identified key roles that students must meet to be awarded the degree, like most documents on the GSCC website, make no mention of combating oppression. The exception is the post-qualification awards in both mental health and child care. The former requires that practitioners provide evidence of 'supporting people with mental health problems to challenge and overcome their experience of oppression' (GSCC, 2006, p 15), while the latter stipulates the need to 'formulate needs led assessments which take full account of the child or young person's networks and communities, acknowledging diversity and the role of oppression' (GSCC, 2001, p 7).

Supporting people to 'overcome their experience', and 'acknowledging ... the role of' oppression is certainly not a call to take to the barricades, but it is explicit that oppression is a factor to be taken into consideration. It also implies the inclusion of such teaching at pre-qualification level, as such concepts cannot be expected to appear as if by magic on the first day of professional work. It is also worth pointing out that, while it is routinely stated that the new social work degree placed more emphasis on practice, increasing the placement days by a third (from 130 to 200 days), it increased the time spent at university by the same amount, the degree being over three years as opposed to the two years of the old Diploma in Social Work.

The impact of 'managerialism', whereby social workers became brokers or 'care managers', is also blamed for removing any critical structural analysis of individual clients' problems, with the problems of deprived communities viewed in terms of risk and dangerousness, leading to the implementation of strategies for correction by way of assessment, control and punishment (Jordan, 1998). Jordan also identified the increasingly authoritative aspect of contemporary social work which has helped to:

> [pull] social workers away from the perception of themselves as brokers of the informal sphere, who humanize and particularize the public provision of welfare, and help strengthen community networks of social support, and

> towards the authoritative enforcement of legal rules and
> societal norms. (Jordan, 1998, p 187)

While he undoubtedly has a point, it is important to remember that
many within social work helped in the creation of a climate in which
the informal sphere was seen as one where abuse and oppression were
widespread.The informal sphere is increasingly viewed with suspicion
and mistrust (McLaughlin, 2007). Also, the concern over the loss of
autonomy and the increase in paperwork and bureaucratic controls
over social workers' activities pre-dates the 'new managerialism' of the
1990s (eg Jones, 1983).

The institutionalisation of AOP

According to Singh (1996), as a result of this backlash there was a
gradual reduction in institutional commitments to AOP. However, the
concept of a 'backlash' is problematic. First, the extent of the 'backlash'
is exaggerated; tabloid sensationalism aside, more reasoned arguments
against these developments were relatively rare. Invariably, it is the
same articles by a small band of critics that are cited as representing the
backlash; the journalists Melanie Phillips (1994) and Brian Appleyard
(1993), plus social work academics Martin Davies (1981) and Robert
Pinker (1993) (Davies' critique, although aimed at the radical social
work movement of the 1970s, shares with the others a concern with
the overt politicisation of the profession).

It is certainly correct to point out how the term 'political correctness'
was used by the Right as a means of closing down debate, avoiding
criticism or of having to justify opinions or practices. However, the
term 'backlash' can serve the same purpose for the Left. Criticism
can be dismissed as either part of the 'New Right backlash' or due to
inherent racism or sexism.A recent example of this is the way in which
the term 'Islamophobia' does not only signify someone with a dislike
or prejudice towards Muslims but also curtails what may or may not
be said about Islam (Malik, 2005).

However much the proponents of ARP/AOP may disagree with
aspects of Sivanandan, Tompson, Malik and Jacoby's arguments
discussed earlier, they cannot easily be dismissed as elements of the
New Right, the first three in particular being active at the time in
grassroots anti-racist work that was not confined to the lecture theatre
or word processor. CCETSW's statement on anti-racism may have
been dropped, nevertheless the revised *Paper 30* still required students
to 'identify and question their own values and prejudices, and their

implications for practice ... respect and value uniqueness and diversity, and recognize and build on strengths [and] identify, analyse and take action to counter discrimination, racism, disadvantage, inequality and injustice, using strategies appropriate to role and context' (CCETSW, 1995, p 18). Despite the supposed 'backlash' some of CCETSW's principles continued to be part of social work training programmes (eg see Mullender, 1995; MMU, 2007). It is worth questioning the current discourse, though, in order to identify changing perceptions of oppression, the state and social worker.

As defined by Dominelli (1988), the term 'anti-racist' is an unquestionable good, with the implication that rejecting her call or criticising the method is merely the expression of covert racism. This assumes that language has a fixed meaning, being 'an essentially transparent medium for the expression of truths' (Turney, 1996, p 8). However, this is not the case. For example, while the term 'human rights' can be seen as a laudable one that can oppose ethnocentrism (Singh, 2002), it has been argued that the term merely represents the new way in which Western powers justify intervention in the developing world (Chandler, 2002). Similarly, terms such as 'anti-racism' and 'anti-oppression' can be treated as logocentric, with little attention taken to analyse what the terms mean, and in what way their meaning has changed over time. It is by use of such a comparison that the contemporary problems of AOP can be best identified.

The changing political and cultural landscape of the twenty-first century necessitates a critical analysis of terms that had their roots in a different climate. For example, talk of a backlash indicates a failure to grasp how these 'radical' theories and practices are now embraced by most sections of the British establishment.

As discussed earlier, CCETSW was accused of being infiltrated by 'loony left' political zealots using assertion and propaganda to exaggerate the extent of racism within British society. Today, by contrast, many British institutions take a seemingly masochistic pleasure in berating their own racist past. The Macpherson Report (Macpherson, 1999) into the death of black teenager Stephen Lawrence found the police guilty of institutional racism. The head of the Crown Prosecution Service is on record as admitting that his service is institutionally racist (Dyer, 2001). According to McKenzie (1999) institutional racism is at the very heart of health care practice. Another report has called for ministerial acknowledgement of institutional racism in the mental health service and a commitment to eliminate it (Blofeld et al, 2003).

The editorial policies of leading medical science journals have also been accused of institutional racism for their failure to prioritise diseases of poverty that affect the developing world (Horton, 2003). The Royal College of Psychiatry and the Royal College of General Practitioners' attempts to improve the nation's mental health with their 'Defeat Depression' campaign was also criticised from within the profession for being institutionally racist (Bracken and Thomas, 1999).

It was reported that the Conservative MP Ann Winterton had the party whip withdrawn for making a joke about the tragic deaths of Chinese cockle pickers at Morecambe Bay earlier that year. Michael Howard, Conservative Party leader, issued a statement saying that, 'Such sentiments have no place in the Conservative Party' (*Guardian*, 26 February 2004). Even football has been influenced, with Glen Hoddle, when England team manager, losing his job after making comments implying that disabled people were paying for sins in past lives. Commentator and former club manager Ron Atkinson was sacked for racist remarks made when he believed he was off air. However much disdain we may feel for these two individuals, the response does not fit with the notion of an anti-PC backlash. In a surreal development, one of the few organisations to deny charges of racism is the British National Party, one of whose members threatened to instigate legal action suing those who accuse him of being racist (*Guardian*, 25 February 2004).

As discussed earlier CCETSW's 1991 statement that racism was endemic within British society sparked uproar. However, CCETSW's 'extreme ideology' is now very much part of mainstream British society. Today, it is not only the social work profession that talks about endemic, institutional or unwitting racism; the police and judiciary are just as likely to make such a statement. Rather than causing a furore, declarations of endemic racism are widespread, and not the preserve of social work or 'loony left' councils.

Such developments can be seen as a long overdue recognition of systematic racial oppression within British society. However, when every agency is flying the anti-racist flag, including those agencies – social work included – that are charged with upholding both legislatively and physically ever more punitive measures on immigrants and asylum seekers, it is time to view the contemporary anti-racist moralising with a degree of scepticism. The issue of asylum is illustrative of how the reinterpretation of racism/oppression and their solution as cultural, interpersonal phenomena can have perverse implications within social work.

Social work, immigration and asylum

There has always been movement of people across different parts of the globe. However, despite its apparent position as never far from the top of the political agenda, immigration control is, in actual fact, a relatively recent phenomenon. In Britain the first legislation passed was the 1905 Aliens Act. Since then there has been ever more legislation and welfare policies designed to control access to Britain, and to its resources if entry is granted.

Immigration policy and debate has focused on who are the deserving or undeserving, genuine or bogus applicants; of ensuring that the resources of the nation are not spent on the 'wrong' people. From its inception, immigration controls and concomitant debate harboured suspicion over the motives of those who came to Britain. As Hayes points out, 'It was the poor Eastern European Jew who was to become the focus for control and in the run up to the first piece of immigration control in 1905, "alien" became synonymous with Jew' (2002, p 31). Soon, there was discussion over whether Jews were really fleeing persecution or simply here for a better life at 'our' expense. Such debate is remarkably similar to the discourse today over 'genuine', 'bogus' or 'economic' migrants or 'asylum seekers' (Hayes, 2005).

This control of immigration can be seen as having both external and internal elements. The external aspect is perhaps the more obvious of the two, being concerned with controlling the country's borders and other points of entry such as airports. The aim of such controls is to restrict entry to those deemed eligible to enter the country. However, the control of immigrants does not stop once entry into the country is gained. There are myriad ways in which such control is administered, and social workers are increasingly being drawn into such enforcement.

It is not only social workers who are involved in the internal regulation of immigration. Identity checks are undertaken by employers to ascertain whether a prospective employee has a right to work, and welfare provision has been continually denied to asylum seekers:

> The 1993 Asylum and Immigration Appeals Act and the 1996 Asylum and Immigration Act accelerated the process of removing from the welfare state those subject to immigration control, both asylum seekers and others. In 1993 asylum seekers were denied homeless persons accommodation if they could stay anywhere 'however temporary', such as a church floor. With the 1996 Act, housing legislation was

> introduced to remove rights to homeless accommodation
> from *all* persons subject to immigration control. It also
> linked virtually all non-compulsory benefits including child
> benefit, to immigration status. (Humphries, 2004, p 101,
> emphasis in original)

It was not until the 1990s that legislation specifically aimed at 'asylum seekers' was introduced, with the 1993 Asylum and Immigration Appeals Act, the 1996 Asylum and Immigration Act and the 1999 Immigration and Asylum Act, each further restricting the social and welfare rights of asylum seekers (Hayes, 2005). In addition, section 9 of the 2004 Asylum and Immigration (Treatment of Claimants, etc.) Act proposes suspending family support for those families who have failed in their asylum claims. The aims of this piece of legislation are: to remove the incentive for failed asylum seeker families to remain in this country; to change the behaviour of this group to engage proactively in a returns policy; to encourage families to make voluntary returns from the UK; to increase the number of removals and to reduce asylum support costs.

Such measures have led to criticisms that current policies are a form of Poor Law for asylum seekers (Cohen, 2001). This restriction of welfare provision has a direct impact on social services and individual social workers. Local authorities are under a duty to inform the Home Office of any failed asylum seeker, or anyone else they consider to be in the country unlawfully (Cohen, 2003). As social workers are often the ones assessing people against the eligibility criteria for community care services, it is onto them that this duty ultimately falls. Surprisingly, the history of immigration and welfare has been relatively ignored within social work, although recent contributions have begun to address this (eg Humphries, 2004; Hayes, 2005).

In one sense, social work involvement with immigrants and asylum seekers should come as no surprise. Given its role in working with those at the margins of society, the disadvantaged and oppressed, and given that immigrants and asylum seekers are among the most disadvantaged groups in society, social work 'support' would seem entirely appropriate and reasonable. Nevertheless, there is increasing evidence that the social work role with such groups is taking a coercive and authoritarian turn (Humphries, 2004), with the result that social workers are being viewed with suspicion by asylum seekers (Khan, 2000). This is unsurprising when, as Collett points out, 'social workers are not expected to work with this client group unless absolutely necessary, but are expected to report to immigration anyone they suspect of being bogus' (2004, p 85).

It is in light of such measures that AOP has recently attracted criticism from within the social work profession, accused of being nothing more than rhetoric, as a cloak to hide behind while implementing state policy. Social work plays a key role in the internal regulation of immigration policy, being obliged to report to the Home Office if a failed asylum seeker, or anyone they consider to be in the country unlawfully, tries to claim community care services. And there is evidence that local authorities are interpreting the 'eligibility criteria' for services that immigrants must satisfy in the narrowest possible way; one Court of Appeal judge lambasted Leicester City Council, claiming that their policies amounted to starving 'immigrants out of the country by withholding last resort assistance' (quoted in Humphries, 2004, p 103).

Asylum seekers are also being threatened with the removal of their children if they fail to cooperate with the immigration authorities. The withdrawal of benefits to failed asylum seekers, under section 9 of the 2004 Asylum and Immigration Act, raised the possibility that children could be taken into care as their parents would no longer be able to support them; a scenario which has begun to be realised, according to one report on the Community Care website (Vevers and Taylor, 2005).

Much criticism from social services departments over the proposed removal of failed asylum seekers was that it was unworkable and the call was for closer liaison between the local authorities, the Home Office and immigration officials. Even the Refugee Council accepted the need for 'enforced returns' (Cohen, 2004). While the British Association of Social Workers opposes the withdrawal of support to asylum seekers, its objection is not one of principle, but on the basis of the extra burden it will place on social services and social workers (BASW, 2003).

Discussing this incorporation of social services departments into the 'asylum removal' proposals, Humphries notes how little resistance there has been to social work's involvement in this process:

> The evidence so far suggests that social workers and social services have a clear vision of what is required of them by social policy on immigration controls, even to the extent of active cooperation with the removal and deportation of people in the most grim circumstances. They have not resisted the gate-keeping and inhumane role thrust upon them. It is no wonder they are despised and feared

by the people they purport to help. We can safely regard
the rhetoric about anti-oppressive practice and anti-racist
practice as harmless delusion. (Humphries, 2004, p 104)

She goes on to conclude that the profession needs 'to stop pretending
that what it calls "anti-oppressive practice" is anything but a gloss to help
it feel better about what it is required to do, a gloss that is reinforced
by a raft of books and articles that are superficial and void of a political
context for practice' (Humphries, 2004, p 105).

Given the aforementioned goals of the emancipatory/anti-oppressive
social worker to reduce both personal and societal oppression, asylum
policies and practice would appear to sit uneasily with such egalitarian
aspirations. After all, all local authorities, and especially social services
have their 'equality' policies and statements, and – as we have seen
– social work training, and by implication post-qualification practice,
has a heavy commitment to combating oppression.

This narrowing of politics to the interpersonal level could see social
workers demonstrate their 'anti-oppressive' credentials by admonishing
the asylum seeker for using sexist language, while at the same time
refusing them services, or taking their children from them, because
they are not considered 'one of us'. Such a problem has come about,
at least in part, because in their desire to make the personal political,
anti-oppressive campaigners became focused on the minutiae of
human interaction, in many cases to the neglect of the wider structural
issues which can give rise to social problems. A focus on the power
of discourse in constructing inequality led to the adoption of the
'correct' terminology, and codes of conduct were put in place to enable
us to relate to each other in non-oppressive ways. In the process, the
political became personal, with the battle for equality confined to the
workplace, lecture theatre or the level of interpersonal relations. As
the social movements from which the drive for equality emerged have
been defeated, it could be argued that what we have been left with is a
new professional middle class who use anti-oppressive terminology to
gain some sense of moral superiority, while simultaneously establishing
more forms of control over various sections of society.

The state of AOP

AOP, like its ARP predecessor, was born, not from a confident belief
in radical change, but from disillusionment with the prospect of wider
social change. If it can be classed as political it is with a very small 'p',
embracing personal over structural change. It is about 'minimising the

power differences in society' (Dalrymple and Burke, 1995, p 3). The power differences are seen as beyond resolution, so the best we can do is to minimise them.

AOP also necessitates a reconceptualisation of the power and role of the state. Whereas Sivanandan (1985) and Tompson (1988) saw the role of the state as problematic, in that it upheld existing social relations that they saw as being ultimately responsible for racist ideology and practice, contemporary ARP/AOP views the state – even more so than early radical social work did – as a flawed but ultimately favourable referee, adjudicating between competing identity claims. The fragmentation of society and lack of collective consciousness has partly paved the way for this more benign view of the state. Where there has been a strong sense of collective solidarity, the role of the state, including social welfare providers, is more likely to be viewed with suspicion (Popplestone, 1971; Bryant, 1973). Likewise, Gilroy's review of the inner city riots of the early 1980s notes that while not all of the riots followed the same pattern, they shared a suspicion of the state and resulted in part because of the authorities 'violating the community's right to control its own existence' (1987, p 241).

In contrast, the fragmentation of class struggle, the concomitant focus on identity and difference, of power as being diverse, beyond resolution and operating at a variety of levels, is more likely to problematise the public asking the state to intervene as neutral arbiter. For example, admissions of 'institutional racism' by public bodies such as the police tend to focus on individual police officers or the 'canteen culture' as the cause of the problem; racism/oppression is redefined as an interpersonal, cultural phenomenon rather than a questioning of the role of the police (Hume, 2003).

Likewise, within social work there is evidence that social work students are more likely to correct service users' language or attitudes than challenge wider issues (Collins et al, 2000). Indeed, Dominelli (2002) sees the role of the AOP social worker as intervening in any 'oppressive' conversation they may overhear, with the back-up of their employer if necessary (and presumably the police if the public fail to concede the argument to the AOP social worker). Focusing on the individual in this way allows the 'anti-discriminatory/anti-oppressive social worker' to observe and police the behaviour and language of people, while at the same time actively implementing inherently racist, internal immigration controls, for example, by checking immigration status, which research found they regarded as merely a bureaucratic irritant rather than an ethical or political dilemma (Humphries and Mynott, 2001).

There was undoubtedly a struggle to get issues of racism and other forms of oppression taken seriously during the 1980s and early 1990s. However, it is clear that the political landscape of the twenty-first century differs significantly from that time.

Taking a stand against oppression in the past brought one into conflict with the state, which stood accused of promoting and benefiting from a society divided along class, race and gender lines. Today, the state and its institutions, increasingly sensitive to charges of discrimination in such areas, publicly acknowledge the charge and promise to take steps to eradicate it. In this sense the concept of a backlash against AOP within society in general and social work in particular is problematic.

Of importance here is the question of who is charged with intervening and resolving these ever-expanding categories of the oppressed. The change agent in these discourses is no longer the working class, and any notion of collective agency immediately encounters fear of abuses of power within its ranks. The danger is, as will be discussed in subsequent chapters, that the subjects of such oppression become too diffuse, fearful and weak to constitute historical agents of change. In such circumstances, it is invariably the state, whether in the guise of the government, police or social worker that is likely to be seen as the solution to the problem of oppression.

To be anti-racist or anti-oppressive today one need not view the state with any sense of suspicion. Indeed, anti-oppressive practice has played a part in allowing the state to reposition itself as a benign arbiter between competing identity claims. Perversely, given its aim to make the personal political, anti-oppressive practice shares much with the moral underclass discourse (Levitas, 1998) whereby the problems of society are recast as caused by the moral failings of individuals who need censure and correction from the anti-oppressive social worker. Surveying the scene from the radical social work movement to its postmodern fragmentation, Langan documents the loss of optimism for wider social change and acutely observes how the move towards 'race awareness training', and other such classroom-based consciousness raising, 'revealed the shift in the attitude of radical social work. A movement which a decade earlier had regarded working-class people as the agency of the revolutionary transformation of society now assumed that the same people required professional training to eradicate their prejudices' (2002, p 214).

The working-class subject in social work was now seen as part of the problem rather than the solution to societal oppression. The anti-oppressive social worker was well placed for personally policing, not politically empowering the disadvantaged. In summary, social work's perception of the subject was as one who had to be viewed with suspicion, the focus of intervention either because they were unable to cope for themselves or because they were, whether aware of it or not, likely to be oppressing others. This notion of the subject carries implications for the profession and the public, which are examined in the remainder of the book.

FOUR

Agency, pathology and abuse

Introduction

The preceding chapters have documented some important trends within social work, in particular the politicisation and institutionalisation of radical-based theories. Without disputing the insights and practical applications of such developments, the point was made that the discourse changed from one where people were seen as active subjects with the means to overcome their oppression, to one in which they were to be viewed with suspicion as they were – whether aware of it or not – likely to be oppressing others. The politicisation of social work was influenced by a general sense of pessimism for wider social change. Whereas many argue that the reaction or backlash against radical and anti-oppressive social work embodied a depoliticisation, in reality it was a depoliticisation within left-wing thought and action that led to the rise of such initiatives.

The interaction of political and social developments on how we perceive not only social problems but also our very subjectivity is further considered in relation to the rise of the discourses of pathology and abuse. Again, the intention is not to discuss these issues in relation to the specifics of practice but to draw out similarities in how they regard people; mainly their tendency to view people as prisoners of their past and the incorporation of wider societal influences on the perception of 'individual' problems and solutions. The specifics of practice may not be discussed but it is argued that there are implications for the worker and the therapeutic relationship.

The standpoint I adopt is one in which each categorisation, whether diagnostic or discursive, is treated not as a discrete entity, but as a category that has arisen due to a combination of factors. In relation to mental disorder the influence of outside events on practice has been well documented. As Busfield notes:

> Contrary to existing medical beliefs, it is not that knowledge as to the precise causes of mental disorders determines the way in which we intervene to deal with the problem

of mental disorder. Rather, it would be more accurate to say that the political acceptability of particular forms of intervention determines *the* causes of the different types of mental disorder. (Busfield, 1996, p 142, emphasis in original)

However, contrary to Busfield, I do not want to give the impression that those in political power are free to dictate the terms or trajectory of the debate. For example, negotiation of the sick role takes place between doctor and patient (Wainwright and Calnan, 2002). The cost of welfare benefits is also an unintended and unwelcome consequence for the Treasury (DH, 1998b), and there has been sustained hostility to recent proposals to reform mental health legislation (McLaughlin, 2006; *Guardian*, 31 October 2005).

Pivotal to the rise of both psychological and psychiatric disorders is the belief that our emotions and behaviour can be categorised, and each categorisation entails a negation of agency as the individual's behaviour is deemed to be outside their control. Their 'syndrome', 'addiction', 'illness' or 'disease' is held responsible for their actions. Such a claim does not mean that psy-interventions have limited their intervention in the past to clearly defined discrete groups of people. For instance, by the 1780s, over 5,000 people were confined in the Hôpital Général, a French asylum. Nevertheless, not all of these people would be 'mad', as the inmates included 'the debauched, spendthrift fathers, prodigal sons, blasphemers, men who "seek to undo themselves," libertines' (Foucault, 1967, p 65), while another French asylum, the Salpêtrière, received:

> Pregnant women and girls, wet nurses and their nurselings; male children from the age of seven or eight months to four or five years of age; young girls of all ages; aged married men and women; raving lunatics, imbeciles, epileptics, paralytics, blind persons, cripples, people suffering from ringworm, incurables of all sorts, children afflicted by scrofula ... (quoted in Szasz, 1997, p 14)

According to Foucault (1967), only around one-tenth of the internees were the mentally distressed. This gives further credence to the claim that the origin of confinement had more to do with social and economic problems than anything else. Interestingly, there was no comparable move towards incarceration in Britain at this time, although there was some growth in the use of private madhouses and pauper workhouses (Parry Jones, 1972). With such a wide-ranging net it is difficult to disagree with George Rosen, who forcefully comments that 'the individual was committed not primarily to receive medical care but rather to protect society and to prevent the disintegration of its institutions' (quoted in Szasz, 1997, p 14).

This adds weight to Busfield's (1996) argument (and an argument of this book) that policy and practice are often driven by imperatives that are hidden within a rhetoric of care. The aim of this chapter is therefore to explore how contemporary discourse and practice is similarly influenced by prevailing political imperatives and dominant societal influences.

The imposition or adoption of a psychiatric diagnostic label has implications for human agency; the diagnostic label can be seen as the main driver of behaviour. Of interest for social work is not only how it has been influenced by – and has also challenged – such reductionism, but also how it has helped shape current interpretations of the causes of individual and social problems. This is detailed by looking at traditional medical explanations and more interactive psychological interpretations of madness. The concept of abuse, it is argued, is pivotal in understanding the exponential rise in diagnostic criteria. Of relevance to social work is not only its relationship to mainstream psychiatry with regards to statutory requirements, which are discussed in Chapter Five, but its role in constructing the subject of abuse.

The rise of pathology

In 42 years (1952–94), from its first to fourth editions, the American Psychiatric Association's *Diagnostic and statistical manual of mental disorders* has grown from 130 to 886 pages and the number of diagnostic categories has more than tripled. One statistical analysis of these trends predicts that at such a rate of growth we can expect the fifth edition to have 1,256 pages and 1,800 diagnostic criteria (Blashfield, 1996). A psychiatrist giving evidence to a Parliamentary Committee claimed that 40% of the nation's children are suffering from psychological problems (Marin, 1996). The Mental Health Foundation (MHF) likewise claims that a significant number of children are suffering from mental health problems, although the estimate is a more 'conservative' 20% (MHF, 1999).

In the US, a 1998 census found that 48.9 million people, 18% of all Americans, are 'disabled' in some way (*The Economist*, 18 April 1998). According to one psychologist, one-third of the adult population of Britain shows signs of psychiatric morbidity (James, 1997). A review of some North American studies found that 80 million people have eating disorders, 50 million suffer from depression and anxiety, 25 million are sex addicts, 10 million suffer from borderline personality disorder and 66 million have experienced incest or sexual trauma, to name but a few. The statistical problem with this is that the number of sufferers adds up to several times the population of North America (Dineen, 1999). Perhaps they all have multiple pathologies! (This was an explanation I heard advanced at a mental health and social work conference when I questioned the uncritical acceptance of some of these studies.)

Correspondingly, there has been a steady expansion of 'talking treatments', most notably counselling and therapy professions and services. From relatively marginal activities in Britain, both counselling and therapy are now very much part of the mainstream. By the early 1990s counsellors had become established in general practice in Britain (Pringle and Laverty, 1993), with 50% of surgeries now employing them (Eatock, 2000). Richardson (1997) claims that 450 distinct forms of psychotherapy have been identified. Today it is common for any television programme that contains a contentious storyline to be followed by the number of a telephone helpline to comfort those upset by the contents of what they have just watched. It is worth pointing out that, for what are essentially medical operations such as HIV tests or abortions, prior counselling is not an option you can easily refuse if you wish to have the operation. Without disputing that opting for these procedures are not necessarily easy decisions to make, the implication appears to be that adults cannot make important decisions on their own without professional third-party intervention. Today, we increasingly defer to the psy-experts or lifestyle gurus to help us in our personal relationships, to raise our children, to cope with work, to tell us why we are unhappy, depressed or anxious.

While there have been several recent critiques of this expansion of diagnostic categorisation of the human experience (eg Nolan, 1998; Wainwright and Calnan, 2002), which build on earlier analyses that identified the authoritarian, disciplinary aspects of this psychology of the self (eg Foucault, 1967; Rose, 1990; Parker et al, 1995), in relative terms they are a minority and have not stopped these explanations, and associated terms such as self-esteem and counselling, from entering common culture and discourse.

The expansion of a psychiatric framework within which more and more social problems were being defined did not escape the attention of the social work profession. With a remit to protect the vulnerable, the social work profession was directly affected by the cultural changes discussed earlier. Issues of abuse and psychological distress, and a critique of the societal inequalities giving rise to them, influenced the profession. However, as we will see, social work professionals did not passively absorb these ideas; they also had a role in constructing them, particularly in promoting the 'pervasiveness' of abuse. This interaction can be seen by a look at changes in the discourse by which explanations for mental distress are sought.

Psychiatry and agency

The emerging discipline of psychiatry relied on Enlightenment theories of 'Reason' to give it a frame of reference. By taking a rational view of 'unreason', rather than looking to witchcraft or religion for explanations, a more scientific study was made possible. Central to Enlightenment theory was the belief that progress was possible only through a rational and scientific understanding of the world, in which humanity was seen as having the ability to control and shape its own, and society's destiny. What was previously regarded as 'God's will' or caused by forces of nature was now challenged. Freed from the dictates of the Church, King or God, humanity's destiny lay in its own hands. The advent of Reason led to a belief that humans could master nature rather than be subject to its laws. As scientists offered increasingly rational and plausible explanations for the workings of the natural world, and the role of humans within it, the Church's authority was relatively diminished (Jones, 1996).

The middle of the eighteenth century saw medical men experiment with more humane treatments for the mentally distressed, and hospitals were set up by public subscription in major cities, such as the Manchester Lunatic Hospital and St Luke's in London. However, the 'treatment' still consisted of the old methods of bleeding, purging, blistering and vomits. It was a Quaker establishment, the Retreat at York, that abandoned these methods and developed in their place a 'moral treatment', which was adopted by a number of the first county asylums under an 1808 Act (Jones, 1996).

The belief in social progress inherent in Enlightenment thought also contained criticism of the worst excesses of industrial capitalism, with campaigns for improvements in public health and working conditions in factories emerging at this time. Early psychiatrists like Dr John Hawkes of the Wiltshire county asylum, writing in the early nineteenth century, expressed the need for social improvements such as reduced working hours and improved education, to 'promote mental sanitary reform' (quoted in Jones, 1996, p 129). We saw in Chapter One how the emerging discipline of social work became involved in administering many of these reforms, and while many medics adopted what could be termed a 'quasi-social work' approach, the history also charts how, conversely, social work adopted a 'quasi-medical' perspective.

Traditional psychiatric practice takes a nosological approach to patients. It seeks to classify patients in the same way that we classify other things; in essence people become objects of study and intervention. Human behaviour, or at least 'abnormal' behaviour, is seen as the result of some mental illness or brain disease. With medical science discovering the pathological basis of diseases such as neurosyphilis, there was increasing optimism that further research would soon lead to an identifiable organic basis for many forms of madness. The German psychiatrist Emil Kraepelin, building on the work of his French counterpart Philippe Morel, defined an illness which he called 'dementia praecox' (dementia of early onset, now known as schizophrenia), in which he noted the progressive deterioration in mental functioning: 'Dementia praecox consists of a series of clinical states which have as their common characteristic a peculiar destruction of the internal connections of the psychic personality with the most marked damage of the emotional life and volition' (quoted in Thomas, 1997, p 84). As science failed to establish a single disease entity for the illness, Kraepelin began to focus on the course of the illness, which was mostly held to follow stages of deterioration, with patients not regaining previous levels of functioning, although his own research failed to establish the inevitability of such an outcome. In other words, neither the cause of such psychic disturbance nor the outcome for the individual could be confidently predicted.

Of course, prevailing social mores also influenced the construction of Kraepelin's classificatory systems, leading him to identify 'masturbation', 'the born criminal' and 'pathological liars' as phenomena of mental disease. He also multiplied the number of behaviours said to be symptoms of dementia praecox; from the sixth to the eighth edition of his textbook on the subject, the number of pages devoted to its construction rose from 37 to 356 pages (Boyle, 1990).

Kraepelin's view of inevitable social and intellectual decline as the key feature was challenged by Bleuler (1911), who claimed to be achieving successful outcomes with 60% of his patients, compared with Kraepelin's 12%. He also argued that symptoms such as thought disorder, flat effect and expression of emotion were the characteristic features of the illness, coining the term 'schizophrenia' to illustrate the disjuncture between thinking and feeling. Other symptoms, such as hallucinations and delusions were, for Bleuler, not key features of the illness itself, but manifestations of it. It was the work of Schneider (1959) however, that formed the basis of contemporary psychiatric diagnostic criteria for schizophrenia. Schneider claimed to have identified two 'ranks' of criteria. The first rank, the fundamental features necessary to establish the diagnosis, consisted of audible thoughts, delusions and feelings of being influenced by things external to the body. Such a scientific/mechanistic view of humanity, with its negation of agency, in effect derogates humanity; for example when one scientist writes that 'we should not ask whether man is a machine but should rather ask ... what kind of machine is man', a belief in human action is conspicuous by its absence (quoted in Szasz, 1991, p 192). The psychiatric patient in such a reading is seen as an object without agency or goals.

Despite being exposed as lacking scientific credibility by a variety of writers over the past 40 years (eg Szasz, 1961; Thomas, 1997), such work still influences the diagnosis of schizophrenia carried out by psychiatrists and approved social workers today, although there have been so many changes to the description of schizophrenia since Kraepelin's time that contemporary psychiatrists would be unlikely to see many patients who would easily fit his prototype. The concept of 'schizophrenia', then, is seen as a social construction rather than a disease entity, with 'evidence' of the existence of the disease being challenged as relying on a tautology; 'unwanted behaviours are taken to be symptoms of schizophrenia; schizophrenia is the cause of unwanted behaviours' (Sarbin, 1990, p 260).

For Szasz (1991), science cannot fully understand human behaviour, precisely because we are not machines, but are endowed with free will, whose behaviour is not only determined but chosen; classifying human behaviour therefore inevitably constrains it. Psychiatric diagnoses are not illnesses or diseases in the way we understand physical illness or disease – as deviations from biological norms – rather they are 'problems in living' that psychiatry categorises in medical terms. It is not that Szasz ignores the different or diverse modes of human behaviour, rather that he has a problem with the context, nature and purpose of the classificatory act. He sees the doctor–patient relationship as analogous to the master–slave one where in each case the 'former member of the pair' *defines* the social role of the latter and *casts* him in that role by force (Szasz, 1991, p 125, emphasis in original). Szasz is often referred to under the general rubric of 'anti-psychiatry' prevalent in the 1960s and 1970s. Indeed, both Szasz and R.D. Laing trained as psychoanalysts, and Szasz still writes on occasion for that audience as a lapsed analyst (Szasz, 2004). However, Szasz' political perspective differed markedly from that of Laing and his associates. Szasz' main problem is not psychiatry per se, he has no objection to people choosing to pay for treatment, rather it is state-sanctioned intervention and coercion in people's lives dressed up as medical benevolence that forms the main thrust of his attack. This position implies that those in mental distress retain the autonomy to choose, which can be turned around to provide a moralistic basis on which to insist that such people should stand on their own two feet and stop adhering to the sick role. After all, if they retain the capacity to choose freely, why can't they choose to refrain from their asocial behaviour (Parker et al, 1995)? For humans, the act of being categorised also provokes a reaction. Echoing Sartre (who was also a major influence on Laing), Szasz (1991) notes that whereas a thing (object) does not react to the attitude people hold towards it, a person does. Cooper makes the same point: 'In a science of personal interaction .... Mutual disturbance of the observer and the observed is not only inevitable in every case *but it is this mutual disturbance which gives rise to the primary facts on which the theory is based*, and not the disturbed or disturbing personal entities' (1967, p 4, emphasis in original).

The main focus of the attack is the way psychiatry likens itself to the natural sciences, viewing the psychiatrist as an independent scientist neutrally observing a passive patient, with diagnostic hypotheses tested and verified via repeatability. However, as people are not objects but individuals with a whole range of experiences, values and beliefs, the repetition of either an individual or group life situation is not possible. The rejection of the brain disease or illness model to explain strange and/or unwanted behaviour led to more social and psychological attempts to understand them.

We saw in Chapter One how psychoanalytic and psychological theories began to exert increasing influence within social work, and how this 'psychiatric deluge' was later criticised for individualising social and material problems. Likewise, more recent attempts at understanding psychosis have had an impact on social work. However, as will be seen below, rather than passively absorbing these ideas, social work has been influential in promoting them, and in turn influencing understandings of psychological distress.

Understanding psychosis

Compared to psychiatry, psychology often portrays itself as the more progressive profession, seeing behaviour as interactive rather than neurologically determined. Yet this is not always the case. For example, Skinner (1971) saw behaviour as reducible to one where stimulus response was the determinant of behaviour, with little, if any, consideration given to independent human reasoning or will. Likewise, Freud's view of psychoanalysis tended to endorse it as a naturalistic science in which antecedents causally determined social events, although, as Szasz (1991) points out, Freud's chief interest was not to classify and control his patients but to understand and liberate them. Freud's work was subsequently used by many psychiatrists/ psychoanalysts to objectify patients in a way that Freud himself did not intend. By taking his conception of the psyche literally instead of metaphorically, the psyche became a thing, an object of study for the gaze of the medical profession that then attempts to classify human behaviour, and in the process 'an introspective psychology is made into a behavioural one' (Bettelheim, 1986, p 53).

Thomas (1997) examines two types of theory regarding causal relations between the mind and brain, the neuroscience (top-down) approach that claims that brain events cause mind events, and the 'bottom-up' approach that maintains that mind events cause brain events. He argues for the need to transcend both theories, advocating a phenomenological approach that considers our intersubjective nature, necessary because 'our understanding of mental state phenomena will not be achieved through measurement alone' (Thomas, 1997, p 171). The act of classifying human beings leads to the construction of a metaphorical prison 'with personal identities as the cells in which men confine each other' (Szasz, 1991, p 202).

Traditional psychiatry, which saw phenomena such as visual and verbal hallucinations as essentially meaningless, being merely symptoms of a diseased brain or mind, has been consistently challenged. In addition, the social mores of the day have been shown to have influenced not only diagnosis but also prognosis.

More recently, especially since the work of Romme et al (1992) and Romme and Escher (1993), considerable attention has been paid to the content of voices, either in an attempt to understand them or to help patients live with them, given the failure of traditional psychiatry to 'cure' them. For Romme and Escher, hearing voices should not be viewed 'solely as a discrete individual psychological experience, but as an interactional phenomenon reflecting the nature of the individual's relationship to his or her own environment' (1993, p 16).

The traditional view of psychotic experiences was, and is, that they are 'abnormal', symptoms of an illness that leads to a descent into madness. This abnormality therefore relies on the assumption that such experiences do not affect the 'normal' population. However, research has found that voice hearing and hallucinations, considered to be second-rank symptoms of schizophrenia, are present in many people without such a diagnosis (Romme et al, 1992). One-third of Romme's study of voice hearers had no contact with psychiatry, prompting him to consider how it was that they accepted and coped with their voices outside a medical framework.

When patients resist attempts to have such experiences diagnosed as symptoms of pathological illness this very attempt is treated as a symptom that must itself be located in a diagnostic system (Laurance, 2003). In mainstream practice such reasoning will be dismissed as a result of the patient 'lacking insight into his/her illness', with one study finding that this 'lack of insight' was the most prevalent 'symptom' of schizophrenia (WHO, 1973). While more contemporary commentators acknowledge the difficulty of defining or measuring the extent of insight, the need to educate patients about it is held to be essential to good clinical practice (McCann and McKeown, 2002).

Romme and Escher's work has influenced many service user groups, such as the Hearing Voices Network and Having a Voice, as well as those psychiatrists who are willing to be challenged and to accept competing viewpoints. Contemporary views on subjectivity may differ from previous ones in which problems in the here and now were blamed on brain disease or illness; the search for such single pathogens has so far proved fruitless despite the best efforts of biological and neurological psychiatrists. However, today's critics can be drawn into explanations for presenting behaviour that are disembedded from the wider cultural milieu. Whereas the illness or disease metaphor is viewed with suspicion, as a construction within which those considered 'mad' are located, a more contemporary explanation is to locate problems in social functioning within a discourse of abuse. The problem does not have its roots within individuals, but within their past relationships. It is within this notion of past abuse that the influence of social work can be best seen.

The past as determinant

The idea that past abuse leads to current problems has become increasingly popular in recent years, with many people drawing on it to explain their actions. Pete Townsend, of rock group The Who, when arrested for using his credit card to access and download child pornography from an internet site, said that he was carrying out research but also that he believed he was abused as a child (while not able to remember any abuse, he suspected that it had taken place). Tony Martin, who was jailed for shooting dead an intruder in his house, may have become a *cause célèbre* for the right-wing press, who railed against the 'political correctness' that saw someone jailed for defending their home, but this did not stop him from borrowing on a popular leftist therapeutic discourse when he blamed his behaviour on abuse he suffered as a child (*The Independent*, 31 October 2001). More recently, the actor Chris Langham cited past child abuse in mitigation for downloading child pornography (*Guardian*, 3 August 2007).

There is evidence of a correlation between childhood sexual abuse and psychiatric distress in later life (Cahill et al, 1991; Read, 1997), with one study finding that 76% of women and 72% of men with a diagnosis of 'severe mental illness' had suffered sexual or physical abuse (Read, 1998). Others point out that too much emphasis can be placed on the abuse as being the single causal agent, when symptomatology in adulthood may be the result of some third variable such as dysfunctional family dynamics (Briere and Runtz, 1987).

One influential text on the subject of childhood sexual abuse and its effect on later life claimed that around one-quarter of children are subject to sexual abuse, and that, 'The long term effects ... can be so pervasive that it's sometimes hard to pinpoint exactly how the abuse affected you. It permeates everything: your sense of self, your intimate relationships, your sexuality, your parenting, your work life, even your sanity' (Bass and Davies, 1988, p 33).

From this perspective, the fact that you may not remember being abused is no guarantee that you weren't. According to Bass and Davies 'If you think that you were abused and your life shows the symptoms, then you probably were' (1988, p 22). Here, a multitude of personal and social concerns can be attributed to past abuse, in some strange hybrid of Freudian theory and social determinism. It is worth noting also that there appears to be an insinuation here that homosexuality is caused by abuse, akin to the 'you're only gay/lesbian because you were abused/raped' school of thought, a belief that can prevent such victims from disclosing childhood abuse (Huntingdon, 1998).

Bass and Davies found themselves caught up in the debate over the validity of memory. Recovered memories of past abuse uncovered during the therapeutic process were held to be accurate recollections of repressed trauma. These incidents, while not remembered, were held to be responsible for the patient's problems in adulthood. To disbelieve or treat with suspicion accusations of sexual abuse, even of uncorroborated and/or previously unremembered abuse was held by some to be further perpetrating the abuse. According to Alcoff and Gray, 'The pattern that emerges from these disparate responses is that if the survivor speech is not silenced before it is uttered, it is categorized within the mad, the untrue, or the incredible' (1993, p 267).

The rise of abuse

Although 'battered baby syndrome' was identified, and in the process medicalised, in the early 1960s (Kempe et al, 1962), it was in the 1970s that child abuse became a major issue for social services following the death of Maria Colwell (DHSS, 1974). It gained further prominence in the 1980s and 1990s after several high-profile tragedies where children died at the hands of their carers, with the subsequent inquiries being critical of social services' involvement and failure to protect (eg Beckford Report, 1985; DH, 1995). Increasing awareness of the reality of child abuse led to pressure being exerted on social service departments to locate and prevent such abuse taking place. This led to later accusations that social workers were being over-zealous in approach, for example in the Cleveland and Orkney cases where social workers stood accused of removing children unnecessarily, with little evidence that they were being abused (DHSS, 1988; Scottish Office, 1992).

Anyone familiar with child protection social work will be only too well aware of the reality of some horrendous instances of the abuse of children. In cases such as those above, the dilemma of when to intervene is crystallised; reluctance to intervene in family life can inadvertently lead, in extreme cases, to children dying, whereas an eagerness to intervene can criminalise parents and harm children needlessly. The main concern of this book, however, is not with the rudiments of social work practice per se, but of what such practice tells us about changing attitudes to human agency and subjectivity. The focus on abuse becomes problematic in that, rather than being viewed as unusual, abuse is seen as a wide-ranging, omnipresent phenomenon. A focus on individual, abusive families is criticised for not taking into account wider structural problems such as poverty, which are held to contribute to child abuse: 'Rather than being primarily concerned with trying to identify abusive families and provide individualized treatment we need to concentrate our energies on primary prevention strategies and wider social reforms' (Parton, 1985, p 187).

This position, which at first glance can seem to acknowledge that the solution to the problem of child abuse lies outside individual families, nevertheless carries the implicit endorsement of the expansion of social work activity into the lives of all families. From a concern with the prevalence of child abuse, social work began to uncover other, hitherto hidden, categories of the abused, for example, elder abuse, domestic violence, satanic abuse, abuse of women by men (and vice versa), abuse of women by women, and men by men. A report has called on the extent of adolescent abuse to be acknowledged, which the authors claim is probably as prevalent as child abuse (Rees and Stein, 1999).The use of the word 'probably' indicates that they do not know the true extent of the problem, but that does not stop them from concluding that it is an area requiring major intervention. The focus on domestic violence by feminist campaigners, initially primarily concerned with male to female violence, now provides a rubric with which all interpersonal relationships can be viewed. According to the Social Services Inspectorate, 'Abuse may be described as physical, sexual, psychological or financial. It may be intentional or unintentional or the result of neglect' (SSI, 1993, p 3). Mullender takes this further, being of the view that:

> Domestic violence will be understood here as typically combining physical, sexual and emotional abuse and intimidation ... by one partner over the other in an intimate relationship. It is predominantly perpetrated by men against women (across all ethnic and socioeconomic groupings), sometimes the other way round, and also occurs in same-sex couples... Disabled women may be particularly vulnerable to abuse, for example when their abuser is also their carer. Domestic violence also forms one aspect of elder abuse. (Mullender, 2002, p 64)

The 'intimate relationship' need not be a sexual one, which then leads to a myriad of potential abusers, for example, sibling on sibling, child to parent, carer to cared and so on. Indeed, according to one local authority:

> A person who abuses may be:
> * A member of staff, proprietor or service manager
> * A member of a recognized professional group
> * A volunteer or member of a community group such as a place of worship or social club
> * A service user or vulnerable adult
> * A spouse, relative or member of the person's social network
> * A carer, ie: (sic) someone who is responsible for an assessment under the Carers (Recognition and Services) Act 1996
> * A neighbour, member of the public or stranger
> * A person who deliberately targets vulnerable adults (www.swindon.gov.uk/textV2/socialcare/social-adultsocialcare/social-adultsprotectionworkersguide/social-adultsworkersguiderecognition.htm)

In other words, everyone is a potential abuser. Mullender (2002) cites numerous studies that claim to show the high prevalence of abuse, particularly, but not exclusively, suffered by women. However, such large claims have been criticised for having such broad definitions of what constitutes abuse, a conceptualisation that is entirely arbitrary, in that the accuser's perception of whether abuse has taken place or not is mostly believed (Furedi, 1997). This privileging of the subjective interpretation of the victim is now commonplace, for example with regard to race, the Macpherson Report recommends that a racist incident is defined as 'any incident which is perceived to be racist by the victim or by any other person' (Macpherson, 1999, p 328). Similarly, guidance to all staff working within the National Health Service, where many social workers are based, makes it clear that it is for the 'victim' to determine whether they have been harassed, abused or bullied (GWC, 2000). Indeed, failure to believe the 'abused' is taken to be further abusing them. According to Furedi, 'By stigmatizing the refusal to believe, the accuser is accorded monopoly over some transcendental truth. In this way, thinking the worst about people is interpreted as an act of courage rather than what it really is – an expression of misanthropy' (1997, p 79).

This belief in abuse invites us to take as fact something that may not have happened, or even if it did, is only abuse as seen through the cultural conditions of today and the loose interpretations of what constitutes abuse. Within the confines of a therapeutic relationship an element of trust and acceptance is crucial to the process. The major problem is not 'the right to be believed' per se but that this right, once confined to the relationship between therapist and client, has expanded into a myriad of societal encounters and increasingly encroaches on the public domain, with the victim's definition being given privileged status. The drive to believe the 'victim' has implications also for those accused of abuse on the mere say-so of their accuser; the concept of 'innocent until proven guilty' is under threat in aspects of this debate. Again, this is less to do with the private, therapeutic relationship than the problem of such private disclosures becoming public ones without corroborating evidence, as happened at the height of the recovered/false memory syndrome phenomenon (Orr, 1999; Scotford, 1999).

A case study: from illness to abuse

The following case study concerns someone who, from Alcoff and Gray's (1993) perspective, has been 'categorised within the mad'. It is useful as an illustration of how such assumptions are relatively unchallenged today, even by those who are normally critically astute. The clinical, campaigning and written work of, for example, Phil Thomas, a practising psychiatrist, has been of enormous benefit in both a practical and intellectual way. Nevertheless, it is possible to pinpoint in his work the move from one discourse, that of 'illness' to another, that of 'abuse'.

Thomas (1997, pp 89–93) cites the case of 'Jim', who first presented to a psychiatrist at the age of 19, following a period of time when his family and friends noted him becoming increasingly anxious and withdrawn. As his condition worsened he was admitted to hospital for assessment under section 2 of the 1983 Mental Health Act, which was later converted to section 3, a treatment order that can last for up to six months, as he continued to deteriorate. Thomas cites an entry in Jim's case notes that summarises aspects of the traditional view of such patients:

> He remains disturbed, deluded and hallucinated. At times his behaviour can be quite threatening, and his symptoms appear to have made only a partial response to medication. In my view he has a poor prognosis schizophrenic illness, a variety commoner in men, probably associated with neurodevelopmental features. He will have to remain on medication for years because the family show evidence of high expressed emotion. Plan discharge over the next three weeks. (Thomas, 1997, p 91)

These notes, made two months after Jim was first admitted, show the influence of the traditional view of psychiatry. The 'symptoms' are clearly held to be due to a 'schizophrenic illness', which itself stems from neurological problems. The inability of medication to 'cure' the 'illness' is acknowledged, as Jim will have to take it for the long term. The content of Jim's hallucinations, delusions or of any voices he was hearing are rendered unimportant. They are, after all, in this traditional view seen as merely the outward expression of a discrete illness.

A year later, Jim's consultant psychiatrist, whom he saw once a year, told him he must continue on his medication despite the side effects he was suffering. His community nurse, who visited to administer his medication, told him she was too busy to discuss the content of his belief system. It was not until a young care worker befriended him, making a point to spend time listening to him that Jim's story emerged.

Jim confided to the care worker that he had heard voices for years, long before seeing the psychiatrist. Encouraged to discuss his past experiences, Jim began to open up more and more:

> He remembered times in childhood when his parents went out for the night, and he and his brother went to stay with his maternal grandparents for the evening. To his horror he remembered being sexually abused by his grandfather, who had told him that if he ever told anyone his willy would be chopped off and his brain would be removed, turning him into a zombie. (Thomas, 1997, p 92)

This incident at the age of nine led to him becoming anxious, withdrawn and occasionally aggressive. Exploring this abuse with the care worker and then a new, more understanding psychiatrist helped Jim to improve his functioning, come off psychiatric medication, drop contact with psychiatric services, and three years down the line he managed to enrol at university. While he still heard the voices, he accepted them as part of who he was, and was able to deal with them. He no longer viewed himself as ill.

Such a successful outcome relied on Jim being seen as a person and not a patient. The content of his delusions (that he was going to be castrated) and the voices (warning him to 'play the game' and that he was a 'dirty piece of shit') are rendered understandable in the context of his abusive past.

This case study can usefully demonstrate the way in which current discourse shapes understanding and intervention in much the same way as previously. If 'mental illness' and 'schizophrenia' do not exist as entities in and of themselves, they can be seen as discursive signifiers, used to label people and behaviours that we do not understand. A dominant medical discourse encourages and cajoles (by use of professional power) people to view their experiences within its field. If you are hearing voices, are hallucinating or are delusional it is due to your illness, and if you are ill it follows that medical treatment under the authority of the doctor is necessary. In contrast, a more therapeutic approach views such experiences as important; rather than dismissing them, the content and origin of them can render them comprehensible. The person is seen as a historical, socially interactive subject. However, such interventions tend to reduce the realm of the subject to a familial, interpersonal zone, which can miss wider cultural influences on the self, and how we make sense of our experiences.

Reviewing the case study, we can dismiss the medical discourse as representing the 'truth' regarding psychotic experience, given the weakness of the concept and the historical, political and social factors that have influenced the profession of psychiatry. Nevertheless, does Jim's account have any greater claim to representing the reality of his situation? In truth, we will never know if such abuse did take place, and indeed there is evidence with regard to memory that would treat with suspicion the idea that we ever remember past experiences accurately (Middleton and Edwards, 1991).

If people draw on available discourses to make sense of who they are, then it is possible to argue that Jim is merely swapping one discourse, the medical one, for another, that of abuse. In a similar way, Johnstone (2000), a clinical psychologist, in her critique of how psychiatry medicalises and individualises women's oppression, discusses case studies where women defined their problems in more psychological terms. Again, however, there is no consideration that the women are locating their problems, encouraged by the psychologist, within a therapeutic discourse that is prevalent today.

It is also possible in attributing mental distress to past abuse that psychology can pathologise at the same time that it seeks a more social-psychological explanation. For example, James (2005) critiques mainstream psychiatric approaches to schizophrenia, detailing a study that claims that two-thirds of people diagnosed with schizophrenia had suffered past physical or sexual abuse. Such studies are used to undermine the notion of schizophrenia as being caused by a biological or genetic fault, and are intended not to pathologise the sufferer. However, again, the uncritical acceptance of the discourse of abuse can lead to the opposite. There is no acknowledgement of the current preoccupation with abuse in society and of how this may influence how people interpret their current problems; by viewing mental illness as being due to childhood abuse James in effect pathologises those who did and those who did not suffer such abuse. The implication is that we view those in mental distress as child abuse victims, while those who were not are by implication suffering from a psychiatric illness.

The concept of past abuse being responsible for present-day problems is common, not only within social work and the psy-professions, but within wider society. Rather than be subject to the 'psychiatric deluge' of the past, contemporary social work has had a part to play in the widespread acceptance of the contemporary concept of abuse.

The abused subject

In a discussion of the false/recovered memory phenomenon, Burman (1996/97) links the debate to a generalised social anxiety in a fragmented postmodern world, where the very concepts of truth and certainty are thrown into question. She also notes that the discussion is framed in such a way that we are asked to choose between the polarities of either abused children or abusive therapists. Complex social relations, anxieties over truth, history and futurity can be subsumed under the rubric 'abuse'.

Of particular interest, then, is not the validity of these opposing claims to truth; rather than their differences it is their commonalities that provide most insight into contemporary perceptions of the causes of individual/social problems and human subjectivity. For social work, there are implications for direct work with clients and, more importantly, for contemporary social work's view of the subject.

In working with clients there are a range of theories that social workers can utilise (Payne, 1997), of which an interpersonal therapeutic relationship is important. For Dominelli (2002), the work of White (1993) is important as it points out that therapists in one-to-one relationships draw on narratives that seek to resist dominant discourses as an alternative way of making sense of clients' experiences, consequently:

> In working with individuals in a therapeutic way, the anti-oppressive social workers' task is to open discursive spaces in which clients can develop their own interpretive story, that is, one that gives meaning to their experiences, and to understand how dominant discourses operate to suppress this story. In other words, it is about validating the clients' entitlement to explain their lives in their own ways and in so doing assist their empowerment. (Dominelli, 2002, p 86)

For Dominelli, this contrasts with traditional therapeutic techniques where the aim is to 'reframe' the client's story in ways that attempt to assimilate it into the dominant discourses. While this is a claim with which I would agree, nevertheless I would contend that a dominant discourse today is that of 'diminished subjectivity'; some 'anti-oppressive' theorists endorse the dominant discourse in the very act of challenging it. Maintaining a critical stance towards contemporary discursive representations of the self could allow the subject's position and contention to be challenged and probed rather than either summarily dismissed as in traditional psychiatry, or uncritically accepted as in much contemporary therapeutic work (Parker et al, 1995).

Middle-class intellectuals have a long history of displaying contempt for the masses, seeing them as immoral, feckless and disease ridden (Carey, 1992). With its talk of equality, emancipation and commitment to fight oppression, it would appear that contemporary social work has rid itself of these previous prejudices. However, the discourse reveals contemptuousness for the masses similar to that of the past. The subject is seen as an abusive or abused one, whose interactions with intimates and colleagues are viewed with suspicion, containing within them the propensity for violence and abuse. Interestingly, as we will discuss in Chapter Seven, the discourse also reveals contempt not only for the masses but also towards themselves; the suspicious gaze also focusing on the professions themselves.

In addition, the subject in contemporary discourse is viewed as at the mercy of many forces, both internal (eg unconscious, genetic or biological drives) and external (eg personal and social relationships, economics, culture and ideology). The vulnerable individual is seen as both a normal and lifelong phenomenon. Within the social work literature such notions have been extended from earlier ones regarding the impact of class, sex or race discrimination and oppression to include a wider range of issues that render the individual weak and vulnerable. This has also led to a broadening of those deemed to need social work help. If abuse is everywhere then the profession charged with preventing it needs to be ready to intervene in ever more aspects of people's lives.

FIVE

The politics of risk and mental health

Introduction

The contemporary individual subject is increasingly presented as one that is not in control of their destiny; rather than agents acting on the external world, the tendency is to view people as objects at the mercy of forces over which they have no control. This loss of control can contribute to a sense of fear and vulnerability, of susceptibility to moral panics and a demand for protection from some omnipresent threat.

This chapter will discuss the contemporary societal obsession with danger and risk minimisation, analysing its effect on social work policy and practice, with specific reference to the statutory mental health field. With the 2007 Mental Health Act (MHA) giving further coercive powers to mental health professionals, primarily because of a perception that the policy of care in the community has put the public at risk from psychiatric patients, developments within the mental health field at both policy level and practice are discussed as manifestations of a wider sense of fear and vulnerability that is prevalent in society today.

Contemporary society, according to Beck (1992), is no longer primarily concerned with attaining something 'good' but with preventing the worst, with the result that self-limitation, as opposed to self-realisation, becomes the goal of both the individual and society. Although primarily concerned with environmental issues such as global warming, nuclear disaster and toxic pesticides, Beck's analysis of society as a 'risk society' has proved influential. His emphasis on the potential element of future risks, on the anticipation of something going wrong at some later moment in time, makes the risks 'real' in the present. In other words, the fear of future loss impinges on our subjectivity and influences attempts to prevent such loss occurring. Clarifying this scenario as 'the Not-Yet-Event as stimulus for action', Beck notes that in the risk society:

> the past loses the power to determine the present. Its place taken by the future, thus, something non-existent, invented,

> fictive as the 'cause' of current experience and action. We
> become active today in order to prevent, alleviate, or take
> precautions against the problems and crises of tomorrow
> and the day after tomorrow – or not to do so. (Beck, 1992,
> p 34)

Beck, and Giddens (1990), point out that while notions of risk have always existed, today they are seen as products of modernity, as opposed to natural risks. We may no longer be at risk of starvation, in the Western world at least, but are said to be at risk from technological creations. This is what Giddens refers to as 'manufactured uncertainty', in that they are 'man' made not natural hazards. The modern era is then characterised as one of 'reflexive modernity', the modern era having to confront its own creation.

It is important to note, however, that notions of risk are historically and culturally specific, with risk constructed differently in different contexts (Douglas, 1992). Risk then can be seen not as an objective reality but as a way of thinking and relating to others (Parton, 1988). This can be seen in the way that the concept of risk and danger has come to the forefront of myriad discussions, from the food we eat (with dangers of BSE, salmonella and so on), to our sedentary lifestyle (causing heart disease and obesity) or indeed our hectic lifestyle (stress, high blood pressure). Interpersonal relationships tend to be seen not as a source of respite and support but as the opposite, as sources of disease (AIDS and other sexually transmitted diseases), violence and abuse, leading to the observation that we now live within a 'culture of fear' (Furedi, 1997).

In most contemporary debates on risk and danger, there is a gulf between the perception and the reality of the threat we face. While the number of children abducted and killed by strangers has stayed remarkably similar over the past 20 years, the public perception is of a real threat to children from predatory paedophiles (Furedi, 2001). The 'at risk' individual is viewed as more object than subject, as someone powerless in the face of overwhelming dangers, as opposed to the active 'risk-taking' subject, confronting, dealing with and overcoming the difficulties and dangers of life.

These wider social theoretical debates have also had an impact on social work policy and practice. Much of social policy has risk minimisation as a central theme, and within social work it is common to note the coercive nature of much of the work. For example, in child protection work social workers are charged with distinguishing between acceptable and unacceptable child-rearing practices, with the focus being on social control, because of a lack of resources that could provide ameliorative care. For Lorenz, this 'residual model' of citizenship and welfarism means that the state, in the guise of the social worker, only 'comes into evidence through controlling assessments and first line interventive functions, while non-statutory services can provide the caring', which leaves the social work profession open to public opprobrium, 'precisely because it is associated so directly with a state that plays very ambiguously with the boundaries of social rights, relying more on coercion than on endorsing civil and social rights for social cohesion' (1994, p 24). Similarly, procedural attempts to reduce uncertainty, especially in a climate where a concern with risk minimisation is all pervasive, are criticised as leading to a situation in which there is little room for professional discretion, as failure to follow the correct procedure can leave the worker vulnerable to disciplinary or judicial action if things go wrong (Parton et al, 1997).

The dangers of an obsession with risk avoidance for the liberty and autonomy of service users has also been discussed (eg Kemshall and Pritchard, 1996; Tanner, 1998). It is pointed out that older people may be denied the help required to enable them to live at home because of fears that they will come to harm. Similarly, parents can have their children removed unnecessarily as workers adopt a 'better safe than sorry' approach.

By focusing on adult mental health, this chapter aims to illustrate the pervasiveness and sensitivity towards risk today. The preoccupation of legislators with risk minimisation is discussed, as is public anxiety over the presumed dangerousness of psychiatric patients and the interaction between the two. In addition, it is argued that the current climate is affecting social workers themselves as they go about their work, leading to a more coercive approach being adopted prior to the introduction of any new legislative powers.

Risk management and mental health

Various strategies and sites of risk management have been utilised at different historical periods. In the Middle Ages the strategy was expulsion and banishment. For Foucault (1967), the site of banishment was the 'ship of fools', said to travel from port to port keeping the insane from the shores. The existence of such ships is debatable, with some claiming it was a metaphor for the banishment of the insane outside the community (Sedgwick, 1982). During the Enlightenment period, rather than expulsion, the risk management strategy was confinement in private jails or madhouses. The Victorian era saw the rise of the asylum system, with incarceration the main strategy to manage the 'mad'. Risk management strategy changed in the twentieth century, with treatment, decarceration and integration, with the risk management site changing from the psychiatric hospital to the community (Ryan, 1996). Ryan uses the concept of 'decarceration' that Scull (1984) coined to highlight his view that the initial closure of long-stay hospitals led to many patients being neglected in the community. They may not have been incarcerated but they were not integrated.

Of course, these categories are not exclusive. Much treatment still takes place within the psychiatric hospital, and there are still some patients who for a variety of reasons will spend many years, if not decades, in hospital. Relatively speaking, though, with the advent of community care, the majority of those who in the past would have found themselves confined in a long-stay institution are now more likely to be cared for in the community. Psychiatric social work was, and still is today, though arguably to a lesser extent, heavily influenced by medical concepts of cure and treatment. Today's 'mental health' social workers are no less influenced by prevailing ideologies; the name change itself indicative of the move away from a wholly medical perspective on the causes and cures of mental distress.

The mental health social worker finds herself located at the juncture between the hospital and the community. Having overall responsibility for instigating and coordinating compulsory admissions to hospital, and for managing the care of those returning from hospital to the community, the mental health social worker can be seen as not only strategy but also the site of contemporary risk management with regards to those deemed mentally disordered.

The mental health social worker

The psychiatric social work perspective has embodied both modernist and postmodernist principles at various times. In its nineteenth-century guise it was concerned with the cure and treatment of mental disorder. By the 1970s there were attempts to find a common theoretical base that social work could use to solve social problems. More recently, the postmodern hostility to 'Truth' has on the one hand given social work the opportunity to challenge a dominant medical discourse, but on the other hand it has also led to other views, for example those of users/survivors, to challenge the social work perspective. There is, after all, from the postmodern perspective no grand theory with which to understand the social world, therefore social work has no claim to expert knowledge.

By taking on a holistic approach, what Barrett (1988) calls an ecological approach, social work may focus on familial, interpersonal or structural components of the patient's life in order to find a kernel of truth in what are otherwise held to be delusional beliefs. Such social work involvement in community care can be seen from a Foucaultian perspective, not as a benign one but as one that allowed the extension of psychiatry's gaze beyond the clinic and hospital and into the social arena; by making symptoms understandable, it served to increase the reality status of psychiatric diagnosis (Parker et al, 1995). It also allowed for more overt forms of control as legislated for in the 1983 MHA, and which are being increased by the amendments contained in the 2007 MHA that is due to come into force on 1 October 2008.

Under the 1983 MHA the local social services authority has a legal duty to appoint a sufficient number of approved social workers (ASW) in order that it can fulfil the legal obligations the Act places upon it. The ASW must have 'appropriate competence in dealing with persons suffering from mental disorder' (section 114(2)). This would generally entail a qualified social worker with at least two years' post-qualifying experience undergoing an approved training course before being so appointed.

The MHA gave extensive powers to the ASWs. They have the power to make an application (if supported by the appropriate medical recommendations) to detain a patient in hospital against their will. They also have the power to take the patient to hospital or to authorise others, for example ambulance staff or the police, to do this on their behalf (section 6(1)). The ASW also has the power to retake and return a patient who is absent without leave from hospital or guardianship (section 18), and the power to enter and inspect any premises, other than a hospital, in the area of their employing local authority in which a 'mentally disordered' person is living if the ASW has reasonable cause to believe that the patient is not under proper care (section 115). If access is denied, the ASW can obtain a magistrate's warrant under section 135, which would authorise forced access.

Under section 13(1) of the MHA the ASW has a duty to make an application for compulsory hospital admission (or guardianship) in respect of a patient if they are satisfied that such an application ought to be made. This section however also implies that the ASW has an equal duty to ensure that the MHA is not used inappropriately: that is, if the assessed needs of the patient can be met in a less restrictive way then an application should not be made. In other words, the ASW's role is also to prevent the necessity for compulsory admission if possible, as well as to make an application where they decide it is the only appropriate course of action.

Scheff's (1984) observation is that within medicine there is a 'presumption of illness', and that due to the seriousness of many of the conditions they deal with, and the consequences of making a wrong decision, the doctor may diagnose illness when none is there. For example, if a doctor has only a suspicion that cancer is present she may make the diagnosis anyway. The consequence of a false positive is viewed as being less serious than a false negative. Developing this in relation to the doctors and ASWs undertaking an assessment under the MHA, Sheppard (1990) suggests that a concomitant 'presumption of risk' in relation to the criteria for compulsory detention in hospital can be identified. For compulsory detention to take place, not only must the patient be suffering from 'mental disorder' requiring assessment or treatment in hospital, it must also be for 'the health or safety of the patient or the protection of others'. According to Sheppard,

> This would reflect a similar dilemma to that of the doctor utilising the 'presumption of illness'. The consequences of failing to recognise significant risk when it is present would be considered far worse than the consequences of identifying risk where it is not in fact present. Hence, the ASW would, when making this presumption, have a tendency to view the mentally ill person as inherently risky – perhaps because of perceived unpredictability – even when the evidence for this might appear slim. (Sheppard, 1990, p 23)

Case law is also clear that professionals should err on the side of caution (Prins, 1999).

There is, of course, one major difference between the diagnosis of physical and mental 'illnesses'. The former diagnosis, whether false or positive, does not lead to loss of liberty or enforced treatment, whereas the latter may indeed lead to such measures and therefore has major implications for civil liberties. Given the powers of the ASW to ultimately detain someone in hospital where they can be given medication against their will, a cultural climate of risk minimisation is problematic. Indeed there is evidence that both policy and practice is being unduly influenced by such a climate, leading to an erosion of civil liberties.

Fear and policy

The 2007 Mental Health Act (DH, 2007) replaces the ASW with the Approved Mental Health Practitioner (AMHP), who will have further powers than the current ASW. The role will also be open to not only social workers but also other mental health practitioners such as psychologists and psychiatric nurses to fulfil. The introduction of the 2007 Act, which amends the 1983 Act, represented the culmination of a protracted attempt by the government to introduce changes to mental health legislation in England and Wales (similar legislation was passed in Scotland in 2003). It followed a 2006 Mental Health Bill (DH, 2006), which was a more modest version of two earlier draft Bills (DH, 2002a; DH, 2004) that aimed to replace the existing 1983 Mental Health Act. The 2006 Bill merely proposed reforms to the current statute. The drafting of all the Bills and related debate around their proposals has been dominated by issues of risk, dangerousness and safety. In the foreword to the White Paper *Reforming the Mental Health Act* (DH, 2000e) the then home secretary Jack Straw is primarily concerned with such matters. According to him, the current legislation was failing to protect the public, patients or staff, a situation that led to the general public having little faith in the policy of community care. This theme was echoed four years later by then health minister, Rosie Winterton, who said the draft 2004 Bill was aimed at ensuring that 'the small minority of people with mental health problems who need to be treated against their wishes, normally for their own protection but occasionally to protect the public, will get the right treatment at the right time' (quoted in *Guardian*, 8 September 2004). On the introduction of the 2006 Bill the health secretary Patricia Hewitt stated that the increases in statutory powers that it contains were essential for both public and patient safety (BBC News, 16 April 2007).

The belief that psychiatric patients pose a risk to the general public is not confined to government ministers. Indeed, one study found that a majority of people now equate mental disorder with dangerousness (Philo et al, 1996), and only 19% of respondents to a Department of Health survey thought that women who had been psychiatric in-patients could be trusted as babysitters (DH, 2000a).

The new MHA and earlier Bills represent an attempt to address the inadequacies of current statute and provide a legislative framework for the twenty-first century. They follow earlier measures aimed at targeting those most in need of psychiatric services, or more accurately, those deemed a danger to the public. For example, in 1991 the Care Programme Approach (CPA) was introduced with the aim of providing a coordinated system of care for those with severe and enduring mental illness (DH, 1990). This was followed in 1994 by the introduction of 'supervision registers', which aimed to identify, by way of the CPA, all patients considered to pose a significant risk of harming themselves or others (DH, 1994).

The 1995 Mental Health (Patients in the Community) Act, which became legally effective on 1 April 1996, introduced 'aftercare under supervision', or 'supervised discharge' as it became commonly known. The purpose of this Act was to ensure that patients who have been detained in hospital for treatment under the MHA receive the aftercare to which they are legally entitled under section 117 of the 1983 MHA. Installed as an addition to the MHA under section 25, it gave professionals legal power over ex-patients in the community, for example stipulating that the patient had to reside at a certain address, and/or attend a specified place for medication or other treatment. The anomaly was that while the patient could be forcibly taken to a clinic for treatment, once there they were entitled to refuse such treatment. It is to this that the registrar of the Royal College of Psychiatrists is referring when stating that supervised discharge represented 'the worst of all possible worlds. The mentally ill will be subject to the power of "arrest" and to no apparent purpose ... The Act will not provide the extra public safety which the Government is hoping for' (quoted in Eastman, 1997, p 495).

There were then two main problems for the government, some professionals and campaigning groups. First, supervised discharge could be seen as a 'toothless tiger', coercive in that it could convey but was ultimately powerless to enforce its will. Second, it only applied to those non-restricted patients detained under the MHA for treatment, it did not apply to informal/voluntary patients, or to those detained only for assessment. It therefore differed from a Preventative Commitment Order, common in the US, which would allow supervised treatment to take place irrespective of whether the patient was in hospital or the community (Bean, 2001).

It is partly in response to these perceived inadequacies that the government introduced plans to overhaul the MHA in the previous Mental Health Bills and the more modest reforms contained in the 2006 Bill and subsequent 2007 Act. However, despite the move from replacing to reforming the existing MHA, the government managed to push through the most controversial aspects of its proposals: the introduction of compulsory community treatment, and the indefinite detention of those deemed dangerous even if they have not committed a crime and will receive no medical benefit from their detention.

The 'community treatment order' (CTO) would allow ex-patients to be forcibly treated (given medication) without having to be detained in hospital. Under the 1983 MHA, involuntary medication can only be given when someone is an in-patient. Once discharged the patient regains the right to refuse medical treatment, which most of us take for granted. Given the often severe side effects anti-psychotic drugs can cause, many patients unsurprisingly exercise this right and stop taking their medication. This failure to comply with medication has been cited as leading to people being left to become ill again and commit acts of violence (Howlett, 1997). The 2007 Act revokes this right, granting professionals powers to ensure that 'non-resident' patients continue to take their medication after discharge from hospital. There are no plans for such treatment to be given in patients' homes, the possibility of people being forcibly injected in their living rooms being seen as a step too far. The most likely setting will be a clinic within the hospital or community. However, if someone knows a refusal will lead to being removed from their home and taken to the clinic, they may opt for the easier option of accepting their medication at home.

The 2007 Act allows the indefinite detention of those who are deemed to suffer from mental disorder and are judged to be a danger to the public, even if they have not committed a crime. Under the 1983 MHA prolonged detention requires that the mental disorder be deemed 'treatable'. According to then home secretary Jack Straw, this 'treatability clause' is 'an impediment to public safety' (*The Times*, 13 February 1999). Many psychiatrists view personality disorder as untreatable, the patient being 'bad' rather than 'mad', and therefore unresponsive to medical input. According to the government, this 'loophole' leaves dangerously disordered people free to roam the streets committing random acts of violence and homicide. The case of Michael Stone, jailed for the murder of Lyn and Megan Russell, is often cited as resulting from this loophole (eg Steele, 1998; Winchester, 2001). Considered dangerous and severely personality disordered but untreatable, he fell outside the remit of the 1983 MHA. The 2007 Act will close this loophole with a masterstroke of New Labour speak. Rather than the patient's mental disorder having to be deemed 'treatable' – responsive to medical intervention – detention can be authorised if treatment is 'appropriate and available'. It need not be clinically effective. What many of us would regard as common sense – if we are to be kept in hospital against our will then at the very least we should expect some medical benefit – the government sees as an impediment to public safety.

Such proposals have attracted widespread criticism from many mental health professionals, including psychiatrists, as well as from service users, campaign groups and civil libertarians. The mental health charity MIND, a core member of the Mental Health Alliance, a coalition of various groups opposed to the coercive nature of the draft Bills, viewed the 2002 proposals as a step back in time, and was not appeased by the revisions in the 2004 version, being particularly concerned that:

> proposals to introduce compulsory treatment in the community have been retained – when they are neither workable nor necessary. What they do is introduce fear and mistrust into a therapeutic relationship, something that is completely counterproductive and could lead to many thousands of people being reluctant to seek the care they need. (www.mind.org.uk/News+policy+and+campaigns/ Press+archive/mhbopp.htm)

Many psychiatrists are also hostile to the proposals. According to the president of the Royal College of Psychiatrists 'the bill will extend use of compulsory powers to a wider group of patients than is medically necessary, thus putting pressure on psychiatric services, and infringing human rights' (quoted in *Guardian*, 9 September 2004). Angela Gregory of the Sainsbury Centre for Mental Health believed that professionals were being put under pressure to 'detain many more people and compel them to take treatments that do not benefit them' (quoted in *Independent*, 9 September 2004).

The human rights and civil liberty implications are extremely concerning. Take indeterminate detention. While such a move may have relatively little resistance if applied to those lawfully convicted of an offence via the normal judicial process (convicted murderers are already subject to an indeterminate 'life' sentence), it is an entirely different matter to have such a sentence imposed on someone merely on the basis that professionals *think* they will offend at some point in the future. In effect, the proposal would allow people to be locked up – indefinitely – not for what they have done but for what they might do, or, to be more precise, what professionals think they might do.

Risk assessment and the prediction of dangerousness is not mere guesswork, but neither is it objective or conclusive (Robinson, 1996; Appleby, 1997). How many people who may never harm anyone need to be detained to ensure one Michael Stone is caught? As Walker (1978) points out, dangerousness is not an objective quality, but an ascribed quality. Likewise, it could be argued that if people are deemed well enough to be discharged from hospital they are well enough to make decisions as to what, if any, medical treatment they receive.

Risk from services

Such measures raise many issues. Not only could people be detained indefinitely as a result of fears over what they may do, rather than what they have done, and for no medical benefit, but those allowed their liberty may find that it is at the expense of their autonomy to refuse unwanted medical treatment. In addition to the civil liberties implications, there is also the issue that the medication given for mental disorder can have severe adverse side effects. It is worth listing some of them to illustrate the potential consequences for those liable to be subject to such treatment in the community against their will.

Extra-pyramidal side effects (EPSE) include:

- Dystonia: a sustained contraction of muscles, usually of the head and/or neck but can occur in any muscle.
- Akathisia: 20% of people receiving neuroleptics experience this symptom. The symptom is characterised by feelings of inner restlessness and the compulsion to move. Some people have described this feeling as though they want to 'jump out of their skin'.
- Pseudo-parkinsonism: stiffening of the limbs, tremor of the hands and/or head, and a mask-like facial expression represent the core symptoms of this side effect. Akinesia is part of the pseudo-parkinsonism syndrome. It includes reductions in spontaneous movements, speech, and motivation.
- Tardive dyskinesia: a syndrome characterised by involuntary movements usually restricted to the face and neck but sometimes extends to the trunk and limbs.
- Anticholinergic effects: symptoms of this classification of side effects may be present, and include stomach upset, constipation, dry mouth, blurred vision and difficulty in passing water.
- Sexual side effects.
- Weight gain.
- Dysphoria: people complain of feeling dull, unable to think, with a permanent hangover. Feelings of being slowed down in body, thought and reduced drive.
- Neuroleptic malignant syndrome (NMS): a rare but potentially fatal adverse effect. The condition includes muscular rigidity, raised temperature, fluctuating levels of consciousness and fast pulse.
- Agranulocytosis: a rare and potentially fatal blood disorder. (abbreviated from Harris, 2002, pp 71–3)

The term 'side effect' is itself problematic, with many patients pointing out that if it is happening to you, it is an *effect* of the drug. It may be an unintended consequence, but the adverse effect is real enough for the sufferer.

There is also the risk of social stigma that follows a psychiatric diagnosis (Goffman, 1963), and there have been several inquiries that have found cases of maltreatment of patients within the institutional system (eg DHSS, 1972; 1980; Blofeld et al, 2003). This risk from services is the relatively unconsidered third risk in a debate that focuses almost exclusively on the risks patients pose to others or the risk they pose to themselves (Pilgrim and Rogers, 1996).

Current mental health legislation already contains within it powers for people to be detained and medicated against their will, a power which Szasz (1991) has attacked as akin to slavery or the Spanish Inquisition. While many may disagree, arguing that there should be, on occasions, provision for those lacking mental awareness to be helped (or treated) without their consent, the new measures undermine humane intentions. For all its faults, the civil admissions criteria of the 1983 MHA made a clear distinction between hospital and community in the respect of compulsory treatment, and also saw beneficial medical treatment as being a requirement if someone is to be placed in hospital for a prolonged or indefinite period. The social control elements of the 2007 MHA are explicit and far reaching.

Community scare

The government is responding, at least in part, to several high-profile tragedies where ex-patients have committed acts of homicide, and the findings of subsequent inquiries in which poor community service provision and failure to take prescribed medication were implicated (eg Ritchie et al, 1994; Blom-Cooper et al, 1995), or where people were refused hospital admission under the MHA because they suffer from an 'untreatable' personality/psychopathic disorder and have later committed acts of violence (Stone Report, 2006). In addition, campaigning groups such as the Zito Trust have been vociferous in proclaiming the 'failure' of community care, publishing reports and studies purporting to show the disastrous and tragic consequences of a philosophy gone wrong (eg ZT Monitor, 1997). Others have argued that mental disorder is a significant risk factor in child homicide (Stroud and Pritchard, 2001).

Following the homicide of her husband in 1992, Jayne Zito set up the Zito Trust in 1995. Michael Howlett, director of the trust, cites studies from the US, Sweden, Finland, Switzerland and Britain, and claims that 'all but one of these studies show that people suffering from the major mental illnesses are more dangerous than the general public' (Howlett, 1997, p 180). The 2006 Mental Health Bill was published in November of that year, one day after an inquiry into the killing by John Barrett, a psychiatric patient, of Dennis Finnegan as he cycled to work (Barrett Report, 2006). The two men were complete strangers. Two weeks later saw the publication of a five-year national confidential inquiry (NCI) into homicides and suicides by people with mental illness, which found that approximately 70 homicides a year are committed by someone with a mental disorder (Appleby et al, 2006).

Predictably, the government has used the reports to justify the more controversial aspects of its Mental Health Bill. As health minister, Rosie Winterton stated that 'we need to make sure that the care that we can provide in the community is reflected in modern legislation ... there are patients who don't continue to take medication ... [and] at the moment we have no power to be able to say that we want people to take medication' (reports on BBC News 24, 4 December 2006). As the NCI report's title, 'Avoidable deaths', suggests, the authors and the government believe that many of these deaths could have been prevented.

Winterton's remarks show either a worrying lack of awareness or a cynical attempt to use a tragedy for political gain regardless of the facts of the case. Linking the John Barrett case to a need for CTOs conveniently overlooks the fact that he was actually an in-patient at the time of the killing. He had absconded from the hospital grounds. While noting many professional failures in this case, the chair of the inquiry team stated that 'The remedy for what went wrong in this case lies not in new laws or policy changes' (Barrett Report, 2006, p 9).

The NCI report also fails to give much weight to the government's legislative proposals. It investigated 249 cases of homicide (and 6,367 suicides) by people diagnosed with a mental disorder between April 1999 and December 2003. This represents 9% of the total of all homicides in England and Wales during this period. The number of homicides by those diagnosed with schizophrenia was approximately 30 per year, representing 5% of the total. There has been no increase from the previous NCI report in 2001, which followed a study in 1999 that found a 3% annual decline in homicides by ex-patients (Taylor and Gunn, 1999). The relationship between mental illness and violence is a complex one, with factors such as drug and alcohol abuse further complicating the matter. In fact, drug or alcohol dependence alone is deemed to be a mental disorder and is therefore included in the NCI statistics. 'Stranger homicides', where perpetrator and victim did not know each other, are rare and have not risen; family and friends are the most likely victims. In other words, the risk to the general public is negligible.

With the government removing long-standing safeguards for mental health patients – such as the right to refuse medical treatment in the community – and introducing powers allowing for the indefinite detention of someone on the grounds that professionals think that individual may commit a crime at some future point, then it seems reasonable to think that the risk assessment procedures are robust and accurate. However, this is not the case. According to the NCI, 29% of those who went on to kill were seen by mental health professionals in the week preceding the homicide, and were not judged to pose any significant risk. At the final contact between patient and services immediate risk was judged to be low or absent in 88% of cases. Long-term risk was judged to be low or absent in 69% of cases. In addition, a significant percentage had had no prior contact with services. Of those diagnosed with schizophrenia, only half had current or recent contact with services, while one-third had no previous contact. Of those deemed to suffer from personality disorder 55% had no previous violent convictions and 43% no previous contact with services (Appleby et al, 2006).

The impact of mental disorder on violent behaviour is complex. For example, someone may have had a psychiatric history and committed a violent act, but this does not necessarily mean that the former led to the latter. Such a causal explanation is too simplistic a way of understanding the situation. Also, someone with a psychiatric diagnosis may commit an act of violence, but this does not necessarily mean that the incident was a result of the psychosis.

Such issues have led to more scientific studies being conducted into this area. One comprehensive review of the relationship between mental disorder and violence noted how methodological problems had clouded the debate (Hiday, 1995). Social scientists questioned the research that indicated an association on the grounds that the patients in the studies were not typical of the majority of the mentally disordered, and there was no comparison group. Summarising her findings, Hiday concludes that 'the contribution to violence of major mental illness, current psychotic symptoms, or threat/control override symptoms is only modest' (1995, p 124). So, in relative terms, a diagnosis of major mental illness is less a predictor of violence than being young, male, substance abusing or substance dependent, and has been confirmed by later studies (Steadman et al, 1998). Taylor and Gunn (1999) analysed records from a 38-year period (1957–95) and found little fluctuation in the numbers of homicides by 'mentally ill' patients during this period. In fact there has been a 3% annual decline in their contribution to official statistics.

Indeed, the vast majority of violent crime is committed by people without a mental disorder (Swanson et al, 1990). An earlier NCI into homicide by people with mental illness found that 34% of homicide perpetrators had a lifetime diagnosis of mental disorder, but this figure also included 'mental disorders' such as alcohol and drug dependence, which together with personality disorder made up the majority of the 34%, and the report admits that 'most did not have conditions regarded as severe mental illness' (DH, 2001b, p 104). So, in terms of homicides, severe mental illness was found to be less of a factor than personality disorder or drug and alcohol abuse. Even in less serious offending the relationship to mental disorder is only modest, and may be partly explained by coexisting substance misuse. Such 'dual diagnosis' has been implicated in aggressive behaviour and violent crime (Crichton, 1999).

The case for a community treatment order on the grounds of public safety also fails close inspection. The medication that would be given under the CTO would be for severe mental illness, not alcohol or drug misuse, so is unlikely to have much impact on public safety. This is supported by recent studies, one of which found that non-compliance with medication was over-emphasised in relation to homicides committed by ex-patients (Parker and McCulloch, 1999). The earlier NCI report could only surmise that compulsory CTOs *may* prevent just two homicides per year (DH, 2001b), while the later report states that 'We have no reliable way of calculating how many homicides [or suicides] would be prevented by a community treatment order' (Appleby et al, 2006, pp 93 and 139).

In fact, the powers contained in the 2007 MHA could make things worse. It is hard to make a case for those assessed as posing little or no risk being put on CTOs or detained indefinitely, and those not in contact with services are likely to be less inclined to seek such help if they are aware of the implications for their civil liberties. Even allowing for the accuracy of the earlier NCI report's claim that two homicides may be prevented, the obvious problem for professionals is: which two? How many people must have enforced community treatment to cover all possible, if infinitesimal eventualities? Likewise, how many people considered potentially dangerous who may never commit a crime, must be detained in order to prevent one homicide?

Scare in the office

While it is not too difficult to expose the government's focus on safety as lacking scientific credibility, nevertheless there is evidence that the climate of fear and risk avoidance is also affecting those at the sharp end of mental health policy. For example, in England the number of compulsory admissions rose sharply from the late 1980s to mid-1990s, from 15,400 in 1987/88 to a peak of 25,600 in 1994/95 (DH, 1998a). While there has been a slight tailing off in recent years, the Department of Health points out that the fall is likely to be due to more accurate recording measures. Also, these figures do not include the increasing numbers – 19,300 in 1997/98 – of those who enter hospital informally but who are subsequently detained under the Act. Nor does it include those who were first detained to hospital as a 'place of safety' (DH, 1998a). A similar significant rise has also taken place in Northern Ireland (Manktelow, 1999).

If we dismiss the possibility that the long-sought but elusive 'schizophrenia gene' has infiltrated the water supply, we have to look for social not medical processes to explain the rapid rise in compulsory admissions in the past decade. It may be the case that one person has several admissions in the course of the year, the so-called revolving-door patient. Poor recording techniques and the 'Bournewood' case will also have inflated the figures. In December 1997 the Court of Appeal ruled that patients who lacked capacity to consent but who were not dissenting could not be treated as informal patients; the implication being that many people who were informal patients should be 'sectioned' if they lacked capacity to consent to treatment. The House of Lords overturned this ruling in June 1998. However, in the intervening period it is likely that many hospitals formally detained patients who would normally have been considered informal admissions.

Arguably, with the closure of many long-stay hospitals and the lack of acute psychiatric beds, it is only when people become 'sectionable' that they can get a hospital bed. The Mental Health Act Commission's first national visit in 1996 found that nationally one-third of patients were detained, although there were wide regional variations with the proportion as high 90% in some areas (MHAC, 1999). Community alternatives to admission may have decreased, although this seems unlikely given the focus on community mental health teams. How the dynamics of these teams influences decision making is also an area requiring further investigation, as nurses working in mental health have been found to be more likely to interpret risk as danger (Alaszewski et al, 2000).

Another factor that requires consideration is whether the climate of fear and 'safety first' approach is affecting social work staff. The social work profession would appear to be suffering a loss of confidence as well as having an increased sense of personal vulnerability. There has been an increase in research devoted to studying the rates and effects of violence on social work staff. According to Balloch et al, the available research suggests that 'a surprisingly large number of social workers are attacked in the course of their work', most of whom are reluctant to report such incidents due to self-blame or lack of confidence in management (1998, p 338).

From July to December 1999 *Community Care* magazine ran a campaign entitled 'No Fear'. The campaign followed the death of a social worker, Jenny Morrison, at the hands of a psychiatric patient, and set out to highlight the 'unacceptable levels' of 'violence and stress' facing social workers. Such is the concern over staff safety that the government set up a National Task Force on Violence Against Social Work Staff, whose purpose is to 'reduce substantially the incidence of violence against workers' (DH, 2001a). The report cites 'disturbing evidence' from the National Institute for Social Workforce Studies over the scale of violence suffered by those who work in social care, which approximates to the findings by *Community Care* magazine (*Community Care*, 22–28 July 1999).

This perception of danger and focus on fear by social workers, in many ways parallels the public and government's perception of the dangerousness of the psychiatric patient. For instance, although a BBC *Panorama* programme on 18 April 1988 claimed that between 1985 and 1988 proportionately more social workers than police officers had been killed on duty (cited in Balloch et al, 1998), in reality the risk of being killed by a client is extremely rare – according to the task force there were seven cases in the 1980s and 1990s, even though social services employees are in contact with approximately two million people every year (*Community Care*, 22–28 July 1999).

When we look at the statistics on violence we also find methodological problems. The high rate of reported violence in the *Community Care* survey could be due to the fact that the respondents were self-selected, so possibly those with most reason to feel strongly about the issue were more likely to reply. A more significant problem is the blurring of what constitutes violence. For the British Association of Social Workers, violence can be 'serious assault' and 'murder', but it can also cover 'verbal abuse' and 'threatening behaviour' (*Community Care*, 22–28 July 1999). The task force accepts that research into violence and abuse has been hampered by arbitrary definitions, but itself uses a wide-ranging and subjective one. Violence and abuse in their interpretation 'is taken to include verbal abuse or threat, threatening behaviour, any assault (*and any apprehension of unlawful violence*)' and also includes 'what may seem like minor incidents' (DH, 2001a, p 2, emphasis added). A similar preoccupation with the safety first approach of the earlier NCI is also evident, the task force's title being *A safer place*.

If you are removing someone's children, or detaining someone under the Mental Health Act, is it not reasonable to expect an angry or hostile response? In fact, a reaction could be seen as more positive than mere passivity, showing an emotional attachment to their children or liberty. However, it is the focus on the subjective nature of 'any apprehension of violence' that gives most cause for concern. On this basis, the intention of the client/patient/family is immaterial; it is the worker's feelings that are important. The reality of the threat may be non-existent, but if the worker perceives a threat then a case of violence and/or abuse it is.

When professionals start to see their clients as a threat, the boundary between risk taking – an essential part of social work practice – and risk avoidance can narrow to the detriment of the people the profession is supposed to empower. Given the professional autonomy and unique power of the ASW (Approved Mental Health Practitioner under the 2007 MHA), such an internal fear, as well as government and public anxieties over the 'mentally ill', poses a real threat to the health and liberty of those in contact with the psychiatric services.

Risk assessment in social work is not a precise actuarial model in which the probability of unwanted outcomes can be precisely determined. Even where attempts are made to provide an 'objective' risk assessment in identifying past behaviours, the extrapolation from that to a prediction of a re-occurrence in terms of high, medium or low risk is not easily quantifiable. As Davis notes, 'interpersonal encounters lie at the heart of risk work' (1996, p 117). However, it goes further than that. Each individual is also influenced by their interactions with wider society as they enter into the interpersonal encounter. It is in this sense that the wider sense of risk minimisation and personal vulnerability can, consciously or unconsciously, influence the social worker's assessment of risk.

The role of the ASW, in theory at least, is meant to provide a counterweight to medical excess, to only apply for compulsory admission to hospital if it cannot reasonably be avoided. Given that an ASW will have made the application to detain in each case cited earlier (apart from those disposed of by the courts), the risk-averse social worker may well be currently in practice.

From a theoretical perspective, the subject under discussion would appear to be one with a heightened sense of its own vulnerability. The general public, the government and the social work profession all seem to feel threatened from many sides. An objective look at the risk posed by psychiatric patients to the public, or the risks to social workers from both clients and the public, does not assuage feelings of being under threat, nor does it seem to influence the thrust of a government intent on pursuing more coercive legislation.

This chapter has detailed some criticisms of current proposals, many from the social work profession itself. The thrust of such arguments is that the obsession with risk avoidance and harm reduction is inhibiting social workers from doing their job properly, leaving them open to public hostility, limiting their professional discretion and putting them at risk of being subject to an official inquiry if things go wrong. Such views fail to consider the role of the social work profession in promoting a climate in which both the public and private spheres are considered as dangerous places in need of increasing levels of surveillance and intrusion to combat abusive and oppressive practices. As we saw in Chapter Four, the pervasiveness of abusive interpersonal relationships is an established theme in the social work literature. The perception of dangerousness is not confined to the media, the government and the public.

Whether from our intimates or strangers the focus is on a dangerous world and our vulnerability within it. Remaining with this theme, the next chapter looks at perceptions of violence, bullying and harassment within social work and its consequences for both workers and service users.

SIX

The subject of stress

Introduction

The general concern with risk and its minimisation, as discussed in the previous chapter, affects both social policy and social work practice; a preoccupation with the risk psychiatric patients pose to life and limb is exaggerated, contributes to societal anxiety, and has implications for policy makers, practitioners and those on the receiving end of further statutory measures. Feelings of vulnerability, of being at risk, have influenced the mental health debate at the level of coercive legislation whereby someone's liberty and autonomy can be compromised because a preoccupation with risk avoidance influences the extension of professional power over patients, and of how, prior to the proposed legislation becoming statute, there is evidence that existing powers are being used to a greater extent than they were previously.

Such a threat, this fear of the 'stranger at the door', of the 'other', is not new, though the guise it takes varies from time to time. Fear of the 'mad', of unreason, has risen and receded at different historical periods (Foucault, 1967); with other groups such as immigrants (Hayes, 2002), the 'black mugger' (Hall et al, 1978) and more recently asylum seekers representing the public image of this feared other (Hayes, 2005).

The mental health field remains the focus of this chapter. However, rather than concentrate on the overt manifestations of control, such as the powers to detain and treat under current and proposed mental health legislation, the emphasis will be on the current construction of 'stress' and how this has influenced social policy and social work literature and practice. While less overt, it is argued that the debate also exhibits the controlling aspects of the psy-complex and of the negative construction of contemporary subjectivity. The intention is to shift the focus from concerns over 'life and limb', and instead to look at ways in which threats to our health and safety are enlarged to include things that could, at first glance, be seen as trivial in comparison, but which can be presented as more universal and insidious threats to our well-being.

By looking at the broadening of concepts such as bullying, harassment and violence, held to be major causes of stress, two main points are made: first, that a construction of the subject as vulnerable, as more object than subject is evident, and second, that interpersonal and work relationships are increasingly portrayed as being detrimental to our health and safety.

The social context of stress

As previously noted, the twentieth century saw an increasing classification and objectification of the psychological realm (Rose, 1985; 1990), with ever more categories, diagnoses and quasi-diagnoses used to explain human experience and interaction. Not only has there been an expansion of categories, but the number of people said to suffer from such problems has also risen exponentially.

A concern with the psychological well-being of the population has also risen higher up the government's agenda. In 1992 the government White Paper, *Health of the Nation*, identified mental health as a key area for consideration and intervention. Initiatives such as the National Service Framework for Mental Health (DH, 1999) and the NHS Plan (DH, 2000c) developed protocols that were hoped to address the declining mental health of the population. Illustrative of this focus on preventing mental health problems has been the rise of the 'psychology industry'. There has been a proliferation of counsellors and therapists to help alleviate the mental distress of the population. By the early 1990s counsellors had become established in general practice in Britain, with 50% of surgeries employing them by the end of that decade (Eatock, 2000). Layard (2005) claims that the main goal of public policy should be to make people happier, and has called for the government to train 10,000 cognitive behavioural therapists in order to achieve this goal.

Areas of life that were once seen as relatively unproblematic are now viewed as the source of psychological distress. For example, at its 1999 conference members of the Professional Association of Teachers denounced school examinations because of the pressure and resultant stress they cause to children (*The Times*, 28 July 1999). Social and behavioural difficulties are also likely to be reinterpreted through the prism of mental health. According to the Mental Health Foundation, disruptive behaviour, bedwetting and truancy are all indicators of childhood mental health problems (MHF, 1999).

In the adult world it is the workplace that is more and more often portrayed as the site of psychological torment. Whether it is the public or private sphere, the world of work is increasingly presented as a source of stress. Its impact on industry in monetary terms due to stress-related absenteeism and low productivity is said to be huge (Cooper and Cartwright, 1994). Social services generally and social work in particular have not been immune to such societal trends, indeed they have been powerfully influenced by the increase in the discourse of stress (eg Burchell et al, 1999; *Community Care*, July–December 1999). Both physical and mental health problems are said to result from work-related stress, although the dominance of the psychological realm over the physical is embodied in the discourse. According to one writer, 'stress is even more pernicious' than violence, and 'dealing with the emotional repercussions for staff is just as important in the long run as getting any physical wounds tended to' (Thompson, 1999, pp 24 and 25). Thompson's choice of the word 'pernicious' is revealing, with synonyms such as evil, destructive, malicious and deadly, it is clearly meant to convey the message that stress is a malevolent force endangering the workforce.

The reasons for the focus on stress is that, 'whether related to violent incidents or not, it can show itself in both physical and emotional symptoms: tiredness and sickness; migraine, insomnia, tension and muscular pain; nervousness and nausea; depression, a sense of failure, feelings of being overwhelmed, self doubt and apathy' (Thompson, 1999, p 25). The tendency to relate ever more experiences to 'stress' results from, among other things, the way the term lacks clear definition. For example, it can be both cause and effect, interaction and transaction, verb and noun. Someone is said to be exposed to the stress of caring for a sick loved one, while at the same time is said to suffer from stress as a result of this exposure. In other words, as one earnest critic of the 'stress industry' points out, stress is said to cause itself (Patmore, 2006).

Given the rapid rise of stress as a professional, governmental and personal concern, it is worth taking a critical look at how the discourse grew and asking what it represents. In view of the power relationship between social services employees and those who use their services, it is important to question the focus on stress, its alleged causes and effects, in this particular setting. The discourse of stress also has implications for how we view each other and ourselves, and for how the state relates to us.

Stress in the social services

Writing in 1994, a leading social work academic, despite noting that 'just how stressful social work is remains a matter for debate' (Thompson et al, 1994, p 17), felt able to assert in the preface to a book on the subject, that it 'is a major issue ... and one which deserves far more detailed study and attention than it currently receives (Thompson, 1994, p x). In the intervening years the subject of stress in social work has indeed received such study and attention, moving from the margins to become a major issue; the profession being increasingly portrayed as one in crisis, under severe pressure, and at continuous risk of violence or abuse, all of which are said to lead to increased stress levels (Balloch et al, 1998; Davies, 1998; Thompson, 1999). The effect of negotiating the public/private divide, dealing with chronically disadvantaged people, issues of child and sexual abuse, lack of resources and increasing bureaucracy, as well as the regularity of being abused and/or attacked, are all held to be factors in the modern social worker's lot. The impact of working in such a hostile environment is often given as the reason for high and increasing stress levels and related illnesses, and there has been a stream of court cases where local authority employees have received damages for 'stress-induced illnesses' caused by working in such a perilous sphere without adequate support and protection from their employers (for example *Walker v Northumberland County Council* (1994) discussed later).

In the wake of these concerns, both central and local government have initiated schemes to address the problem, for example setting up a National Task Force on Violence Against Social Care Staff, whose aim is to create a safer place for employees (DH, 2001a), and the introduction of workplace counselling schemes in many local authorities. Also, as discussed in Chapter Five, there was the *Community Care* campaign called No Fear, which aimed to highlight and address the violence and stress facing social care workers today. These initiatives are presented as progressive moves to minimise the exposure to stress and violence and to alleviate the consequences of the exposure when such situations arise.

While definitions of stress vary, it is commonly held that it is a negative state (Arroba and James, 1987; Thompson et al, 1994; Wilmott, 1998). For Wilmott it 'can be defined as an individual's reaction to too much pressure. The situation creating the pressure does not seem to be avoidable. The reaction will be negative, professionally and personally' (1998, p 22).

Such authors do not deny that in life we will face demands and burdens that can be motivational and rewarding, but this they refer to as 'strain' or 'pressure'. It is when 'the level of pressure becomes harmful, counterproductive or in any way negative, [that] the term "stress" becomes applicable' (Thompson et al, 1994, p 2). Stress is also noted to be both an objective and subjective phenomenon, 'as it hinges on both the objective dimension – the level of pressure – and the subjective dimension of the individual's response to such pressure' (Thompson et al, 1994, p 3). The role of human subjectivity in the construction of stress is acknowledged. Individuals respond differently to different situations: what may be a source of stress for one worker may not be given a second thought by a colleague.

The 1990s saw a steady rise in concern with stress, not least as a result of some high-profile cases where employees successfully sued their authority for the impact of stress-induced illnesses. Perhaps the defining moment was the case of *Walker v Northumberland County Council* (1994). Mr Walker, a social services manager was dismissed in 1988 on the grounds of permanent ill health. He took the authority to court, claiming that they had failed in their duty of care owed to him under common law. Too much work and the stressful nature of it (he was manager of a child protection team) were held to be contributing factors in his illness. The court ruled that Northumberland County Council, being aware of Mr Walker's vulnerability, had failed in its duty of care; he had already had a breakdown and been provided with support on his return, but this was held to have been inadequate and therefore contributed to the second breakdown, which then led to his dismissal. He received £175,000 in compensation. Other cases followed: for example a home care manager was awarded over £60,000 in another out-of-court settlement in 1999, and the same year a housing officer with Birmingham City Council was awarded compensation for the stress-related illness said to have been caused by facing hostile tenants without being properly trained. The subject of stress and its consequences was now something that local authorities could no longer afford to ignore. Wilmott (1998) notes that this led to many councils implementing stress management schemes designed to identify stress-inducing factors and to develop staff awareness of its causes and symptoms. Despite such pre-emptive steps, claims for stress-induced illnesses continue (*Guardian*, 4 September 2001; Kenny, 2007).

Since the Walker case there has also been an increase in 'empirical' research and academic discussion on the level or effect of stress in social work. From 1981 to 1994 Balloch et al (1998) cite only five such studies. Since then however, there has been an increased focus on stress in the social services (eg Thompson et al, 1994; Caughey, 1996; Collings and Murray, 1996; Balloch et al, 1998; Davies, 1998; Balloch et al, 1999) plus the aforementioned No Fear campaign and the government task force appointed to address the situation. These focus on both the physical effects of stress, and of the stress that can result from being subject to violence. In addition, living with the threat and fear of violence is said to be a cause of stress to staff. According to Polly Neate, then editor of *Community Care*, the level of violence, abuse and stress suffered by social workers is of 'horrifying' proportions (*Community Care*, 22–28 July 1999). Likewise, discussing the launch of the campaign for safety in social work one writer feels able to claim that 'social work today is surrounded by violence, actual or threatened' (Valios, 1999, p 12).

Perhaps unsurprisingly given such reported hazards, personal stress levels among social workers were found to be 'fairly severe' for 38%, 'very severe' for 9% and 'unbearably severe' for 2% of respondents (*Community Care*, 2–28 September 1999). According to one study of fieldworkers and administrative workers, 72% of the sample had scores indicating psychiatric morbidity (Caughey, 1996). It is not necessary to be on the frontline to succumb to such morbidity; even social work lecturers are supposedly affected, with one study claiming that one-quarter were suffering from borderline levels of anxiety and depression (Collins and Parry-Jones, 2000).

Neither is it necessary for violence or abuse to occur face to face. For Wilmott, 'abuse may also come in the form of telephone calls and letters', and he notes that most local authorities include racist and sexist abuse as forms of verbal abuse, and how 'it is rare for a social worker not to have been subjected to any of the above and, as a consequence, have *suffered* some psychological effect' (1998, p 24, emphasis added). It is indeed rare for some sort of psychological effect not to have taken place, but Wilmott's use of the word 'suffered' indicates that he sees this as being a negative and potentially damaging experience. Such a view of the social worker reveals the perception of the individual subject as one with a diminished capacity to overcome unwelcome and/or adverse situations. Indeed, by looking at the issue of 'bullying', we can see that not only has there been a change in how we view children, but also in how we view adults.

The subject of bullying

According to Esther Rantzen of children's charity ChildLine, childhood bullying is now a 'national crisis' (*Guardian*, 6 November 2001), while Cherie Booth, wife of the former prime minister Tony Blair, informs us that bullying has permeated British culture (*Observer*, 4 November 2001). This apparent epidemic of bullying is implicated in research that claims that one in five of our children is suffering from mental health problems (MHF, 1999). Neither are these problems fleeting: according to the MHF they can lead to severe problems in adulthood, which may partly explain why other mental health charities such as MIND inform us that one in four adults will experience psychological distress (see MIND's website, www.mind.org.uk). The issue of bullying in school has also attracted increasing academic attention (eg Besag, 1989; Boulton and Underwood, 1992), and schools are now not only obliged to prevent bullying, but are also required to have anti-bullying strategies in place (DfES, 2000).

In 2003 government ministers announced a £470 million 'behaviour and attendance' programme, with the main aim being to combat school bullying by funding and providing training in 'anti-bullying strategies', with specialist consultants employed to help local education authorities tackle the problem (*Community Care*, 29 August 2003). The social work magazine *Community Care* has given the issue increasing coverage. My own search of their website with the keyword, 'bullying', revealed 1,720 articles or reports on the subject (www.communitycare.co.uk, search undertaken on 5 October 2007).

Specialist social workers are now employed in many schools, part of their remit being to deal with the problem of bullying. Increasingly, social work training programmes are getting involved in 'anti-bullying' strategies, schools are providing social work student placements, and the students are providing a direct link to statutory child care services, a move welcomed for, among other things, getting social work input into areas where families are resistant and mistrustful of social work (Parker et al, 2003).

It can be seen that the issue of bullying in school, something that has probably always gone on, has moved up the contemporary political agenda. However, it is difficult to know how prevalent the problem is, or if it has increased in recent years. Indeed, the view that school bullying is now a national epidemic is sustained by a viewpoint in which any trivial, if unpleasant, encounter between children is seen as potentially damaging. For example, according to ChildLine's website, bullying need not be confined to physical or verbal intimidation, but can include 'being mean to someone' or 'teasing or calling names' (www.childline. org.uk). The social work media endorses this viewpoint. *Community Care*'s 2003 online report 'The bigger picture on bullying' includes 'having rumours spread about you' and 'being ignored and left out' as incidents of bullying (www.communitycare.co.uk). With such a wide range of 'bullying' interactions, perhaps it is no surprise that the report can state that, from 1997 to 2003, 'bullying' was the biggest single reason for children calling the telephone helpline ChildLine.

It is this conflation of the relatively trivial, if unpleasant, childish interactions with rarer, more serious physical assaults and threats that allow claims of a 'national epidemic' of bullying to be made. For example, while a ChildLine-sponsored report can claim that over half of year five and 28% of year eight pupils claimed to have been bullied, the most common form of 'bullying' was name calling, with receiving nasty text messages by mobile phone also prevalent (Oliver and Candappa, 2003). There is also an assumption that the problem is much greater than reported, with the Department for Education and Employment warning that 'Low report rates should not themselves be taken as proof that bullying is not occurring' (DfEE, 1999, p 25). The phrase 'absence of evidence is not evidence of absence' springs to mind here. Nevertheless, the headline-grabbing incidents in which children have killed themselves and in which bullying is cited as the main or contributory factor are thankfully rare.

This perception of children as unable to cope with the rigours of growing up without intense multidisciplinary support is a recent phenomenon. In the not too distant past, the ability of children to cope with the more mundane aspects of growing up, as well as extreme tragedy, was viewed more positively. When a coal tip avalanche buried a school in the Welsh village of Aberfan in 1966, killing 116 children and 28 adults, the surviving schoolchildren resumed their studies within two weeks, and the children and the community were later reported to have coped remarkably well with little outside help. Commenting on this, Furedi notes how today:

> such a response to a major disaster would be unthinkable. There would be an automatic assumption that every survivor in the area was deeply traumatised and inevitably scarred for life. Sending young pupils back to school so soon after a tragedy would be scorned as bad practice. The very attempt by the community to cope through self-help would be denounced as misguided, since such victims could not be expected to deal with such problems on their own. (Furedi, 2004, p 19)

Today, normal school life, from teasing and name calling to making and losing friends, can be viewed as inherently harmful and in need of adult, professional intervention. Indeed, in their foreword to the Oliver and Candappa (2003) report, *Tackling bullying*, ChildLine chair Esther Rantzen and Ivan Lewis, then parliamentary under secretary of state, find it incredible that 'bullying', or presumably negotiating relationships without expert help, was at one time seen as a natural part of growing up.

Of course children do need guidance and socialisation, and schools have a role to play in this, but increasingly a soft therapeutic ethos is being promoted with which children are encouraged to view their interactions and experiences. The influence of the psy-complex is evident in the groupwork, circle time and confessional sessions children are encouraged to attend (and there is often a good deal of pressure for them to do so), where there is a focus on the psychological harm or low self-esteem that are said to affect both victim and perpetrator (Oliver and Candappa, 2003). The issue of school bullying has also allowed more surveillance of children and their parents by the authorities, with social workers, the police and psychologists responsible for establishing a new code of behaviour to be followed.

While such changes are instructive in how society views children's interactions, vulnerability and resilience, this chapter is more concerned with how the subject of bullying is relayed into adult–adult relations, particularly within social work. Of particular interest is the speed with which bullying, a term that in the recent past was mostly, if not exclusively, confined to the school playground, has now permeated the adult world.

Adult bullying

While, increasingly, children are being encouraged to view unpleasant interactions with their peers as 'bullying', the incorporation of such a discourse into the adult world, and especially workplace relations is revealing. Viewed through the eyes of the therapeutic gaze, the perception of adults' capability to negotiate their relationships is increasingly compromised. There has been a growing focus on the subject of bullying within society, the general workforce (eg Field, 1996; Clifton and Serdar, 2000), and within social work organisations (eg Randall and Parker, 2000; Collins, 2001). Workplace relations are presented as the source of much distress, resulting in an explosion of stress-related problems of a physical and/or mental nature. One reason given for workplace distress is the problem of bullying. Peer bullying, particularly of a sexual nature, is said to be a significant problem (Field, 1996; Stevens, 1999).

The culture of an organisation is held to be a factor in the perpetuation of bullying. Frequent organisational changes and the uncertainty it causes, unsupportive supervision, excessive workloads, lack of involvement in decision making and little in the way of guidance or policies to address the issue are all held to be conducive to a bullying culture, according to the Manufacturing, Science and Finance union (cited in Collins, 2001). Cambridgeshire social workers said bullying behaviour by management lay behind some of the failures that led to the death of six-year-old Rikki Neave at the hands of his mother (Kenny, 2007).

Bullying is differentiated from harassment. Whereas bullying is seen as being individualistic in nature and as such 'can happen to anyone regardless of their background or position in society' (Thompson, 2000, p 13), harassment is generally held to be linked to forms of inequality along, for example sex and race lines. Guidance for NHS staff, defines harassment as:

> any conduct based on age, sex, sexual orientation, gender assignment, disability, HIV status, race, colour, language, religion, political, trade union or other opinion or belief, national or social origin, association with a minority group, domestic circumstances, property, birth or other status, which is not reciprocated or wanted and which affects the dignity of men and women at work. (www.wknhssct. nhs.uk/pdf/publications/foi/ashfordpct/policies_and_ procedures/Dignity_at_Work_Policy.pdf)

Just in case we do not get the picture from such an all-encompassing definition, we are also given a range of 'harassing behaviours' that we are informed are 'not exhaustive', which include (and I have abbreviated them here): 'using offensive language or innuendo; sexist, racist or patronising remarks; telling racist, sectarian or sexually suggestive jokes; inappropriate or intimate questioning; name calling, including personal comments about physical looks; language that belittles a person's abilities; spreading malicious rumours or hurtful gossip ...' (www.wknhssct.nhs.uk/pdf/publications/foi/ashfordpct/policies_and_ procedures/Dignity_at_Work_Policy.pdf).

The distinction between harassment and bullying gives bullying its universalising quality. By defining it as individual in nature, one need not be a member of a minority group to be a victim; black or white, male or female, hetero- or homosexual, able bodied or disabled, we can all be united under the bullying banner. This can be illustrated by the wide range of instances that have been defined as bullying. Drawing on the work of Field (1996) and Clifton and Serdar (2000), Collins cites the following examples of bullying behaviour pertaining to social work staff:

Constant criticism, often of a trivial nature, that cannot be justified or reconciled with reality; Marginalising people, over-ruling their ideas, and dismissing their contributions as unimportant or irrelevant; Humiliation by belittling, demeaning and patronising people, especially in front of others; Reassigning work to others un-necessarily and unexpectedly; Undermining a person's authority to carry out their work; Withholding knowledge, information, and consent that people need to carry out their duties; Overburdening someone with work and perhaps setting unrealistic conditions and deadlines; Setting impossible objectives or time scales and changing them without good reason – setting people up to fail; Taking undeserved credit, but not accepting responsibility when things go wrong; Spreading malicious rumours, gossip and falsehood; Not recognising positive contributions and achievements, which do not receive any reward; Isolating and separating a person from colleagues, for example, in relation to positioning of desks, offices or social events; The lack of any opportunity to discuss or resolve criticisms; Subjecting someone to verbal or written warnings imposed for trivial or fabricated reasons without proper investigation. (Collins, 2001, pp 32–3)

Unsurprisingly, given its apparent ubiquity, Collins feels able to state categorically that 'The impact of bullying is considerable' (2001, p 33) and to echo Field's claim that 'workplace bullying is ... the second greatest social evil after child abuse' (1996, p 1). Third world poverty and famine, immigration and asylum policy, rape, legislation allowing the indefinite detention without trial or charge for 'terrorist' suspects and 'dangerous psychopaths', all rendered insignificant when compared to the instances of 'bullying' cited above.

In this reading, social workers are infantilised and workplace tensions recast as bullying. According to Nushra Mansuri, professional officer of the British Association of Social Workers, adult bullying is similar to child abuse, which leads her to view adult social workers as little more than overgrown children (*Community Care*, 23 August 2007). Being marginalised, humiliated and belittled or being the subject of malicious rumours, gossip and falsehood may be unpleasant, and in the school playground may (or may not) need adult intervention; in the adult world, however, they are incidents that have only recently been held to be harmful to our mental well-being. Likewise, 'overburdening someone with work', 'setting impossible objectives or time scales' and 'subjecting someone to verbal or written warnings', here seen as incidents of 'bullying', would in the past have been viewed as exploitation or oppressive management.

Indicative of the newness of the child and adult 'bullying' phenomenon is the references of recent papers on the subject. Rayner's (1997) paper lists 16 references, only three of which pre-date the 1990s, with the earliest being 1985, while Tehrani (2004) cites 26 references, again of which only three pre-date 1990; evidence, not for an expansion in bullying, but in how we interpret social and interpersonal interactions. This change is instructive in what it tells us about views of the human subject and attitudes to resilience; the behaviours have not changed, rather it is how we experience and interpret them today that is significant.

The assumption of vulnerability

While the subjective nature of bullying, harassment and the consequent stress they are said to cause is acknowledged, it is interesting that this trust in the subjective interpretation of events bestowed on staff does not include when staff stray from the therapeutic path and declare that they can cope. According to Ros Lobo, a 'mental health specialist' in London, 'targeting the well rather than the ill is vital. Effective prevention should include ... ensuring workplaces are mental health friendly' (quoted in *Guardian*, Society, 11 December 1996), while the problem for Steele (1998) is the rejection of weakness that she sees as being embedded in the British work ethic. For McLean, individuals' perceptions of the stress they are under is not reliable:

> People are not always clear what they mean by stress. If you ask staff whether they have experienced stress there are some people who want to emphasise how hard the work is, and there are others who want to emphasise how well they are. Some people who are experiencing high stress levels may not even be aware that they are. (quoted in Rickford, 1999, p 23)

In other words, those who appear to be coping are assumed to be in denial. Indeed, resilience is held to be part of the problem (Thompson et al, 1994). Resilience, once considered a valuable attribute has, from this perspective, been transformed into a problematic one.

That high levels of stress lead to high rates of sick leave is taken as given by *Community Care*'s No Fear campaign. The assumption is that high stress levels will lead to physical or mental health problems that will necessitate absence due to ill health. However, neither proposition is as clear cut as the campaign would have us believe. While it is assumed to be self-evident that stress and sick leave are related, the evidence base for this is contentious. Although some have suggested an association, others (eg Gibson et al, 1989; Caughey, 1996) found that, despite expecting that absenteeism would be high, in fact they found any link to be negligible. One long-term study found high absenteeism (defined as over 10 days in a year) to be rarely sustained by individual workers over a number of years (Balloch et al, 1999).

This preoccupation with violence, abuse and resultant stress has only occurred in recent years. As recently as 1996 it did not have the same dominance as it does today. For example, in a sample of 243 social workers Collings and Murray (1996) found that violence was not a factor given by them as a cause of stress. Another survey of 1,391 social worker respondents found that while 687 had considered leaving the profession, 400 citing stress as a factor, 387 frustration due to lack of resources, 210 too much work, only 72 gave violence as a factor (cited in Kutek, 1998). Neither were racism or sexism considered to be major stress-inducing factors. It was the pressure involved in planning and reaching work targets that emerged as the greatest predictor of stress.

Balloch et al's (1999) work concurs, with one of the researchers stating 'Most stress was caused by lack of resources and inability to provide the standard of service staff would like' (McLean, 1999, p 83). In relation to violence, 'social work staff were less inclined to say they had been affected by the [most recent] violence, and residential workers were more likely to say that they had not been affected at all' (Balloch et al, 1999, p 101).

Despite this, what is telling about the present discussion is the emphasis on how weak and vulnerable are social care staff. This negation of staff's ability to cope with adversity, and the imposition of measures that emphasise this weakness such as counselling, tellingly downplay other factors such as lack of resources and staff shortages, which are actually cited as causing most frustration during the course of the work. For some (eg Patmore, 2006), this risk-averse approach to stress, where it is to be avoided at all costs merely escalates the problem. Patmore cites 'stress phobia', not stress, as the main danger to the individual and society. As we increasingly fear new and challenging situations and defer to the stress management experts, our agency is reduced and our dependence increased.

It is illuminating to note that the focus of intervention in recent years has been on the issues that problematise clients and colleagues (bullying/harassment/violence/abuse), and emphasise the vulnerable worker (counselling/sick leave), while issues cited as causing most stress such as a lack of resources and poor quality of service provision are relatively ignored. Indeed it is possible to make the case that a problem is being amplified (violence and anxiety = stress), and that this ignores issues such as the poor services and lack of resources cited as major tensions by professionals in the field. There is also a danger that service users and those close to them, many already very disadvantaged, are being stigmatised for not passively accepting their plight.

This sense of vulnerability, and of positioning service users as the dangerous other that is prominent today, marks a change from the past when tensions in the role existed but were expressed differently. For example, a cursory glance through some old social work texts finds that the subject of stress and violence were discussed, but the overwhelming emphasis was on how both affected the clientele and on how social workers could help them through such difficulties. Irvine (1978), past editor of both the *British Journal of Psychiatric Social Work* and *International Social Work*, in a collection of her works from between 1951 and 1974 discusses the issues raised by exposure to stress and risk in relation to children at risk, parental psychosis and other forms of casework. The focus is on the problems facing the service users and their families caused by poverty, ill health, violence, psychiatric and psychological problems. When workers' anxiety is acknowledged, the focus is not on the client as the source, but rather on the danger of worker anxiety hindering an objective analysis of the situation. Likewise, Davies (1981) discusses risk at numerous points but not in relation to risk faced by social workers, and again 'stress' is not indexed.

The sense of vulnerability and crisis palpable today was not so evident in a time when there was a more optimistic sense that societal problems could be overcome. Miles (1981) noted that Parsons' 1951 identification of Western societies being in a stage of indefinite progress, had 30 years later become a general belief that 'more advances, more inventions, more wealth, would lead to a situation where fewer and fewer difficulties would have to be borne' and social workers' advice was to 'enjoy what you do' in 'a climate of expectation' (Miles, 1981, p 193). The optimism of this period is apparent in Huxley's belief that 'existence can be improved, that vast untapped possibilities can be increasingly realised, that greater fulfilment can replace frustration' (quoted in Davies, 1981, p 4). It is difficult to locate such optimism today and rather than seeing clients as capable of change there is a tangible sense that the disadvantaged constitute an 'other' who pose a risk to social workers' physical and mental health.

It is, though, important not to overstate the sense of optimism. As discussed in Chapter Two, the politicisation of social work from the 1970s onwards, when it was seen as a vehicle for radical social transformation, in reality masked radical pessimism for wider political change. However, when compared to today, such pessimism can appear optimistic.

Without disputing that recent changes within the profession have affected the workforce, social work has never had a 'golden age' free from the tensions and pressures inherent in the role. That stress levels are high and increasing is taken as read, but how is this known? It is not possible to compare the stress levels of a social worker today with those of 20 years ago, never mind 50 to 100 years ago. The authors of the most comprehensive work yet on the subject of stress in social work have to concede that it is not known whether levels of violence or stress are higher now than they were in the past, although they claim that anecdotal evidence suggests rising levels of stress are evident (Balloch et al, 1999). Nevertheless, the fact that people claim it is higher does not mean that it is. A more likely explanation is that the workforce have internalised the dominant psychological discourse in contemporary society. Office politics, sometimes petty, annoying and occasionally abusive but something most people coped with, can now be construed as bullying, harassment and stress inducing. It is unlikely that the behaviours have worsened, given the plethora of codes of conduct, harassment procedures and awareness information that inhabit local authorities today; however, people are encouraged to reinterpret these experiences through a psychological framework of how detrimental to their mental health it has been.

Constructing the stressed subject

There is another way of viewing stress: as metaphor carried in discourse rather than as a simple physiological response. Newton argues that 'the ability to "express" stress clearly depends on the ability to learn the language of stress and the parameters of the stress discourse' (1999, p 243). For him, the 'colonizing power of stress' has been matched by few other discourses that the social or medical sciences have presented us with (Newton, 1999, p 244). What concerns Newton is 'not just why we believe in the reality of stress, but why we believe in current representations of stress' (1999, p 244). In other words, stress can be seen as a metaphor for wider social and cultural concerns. 'Stress', then, is not an entity in and of itself, but is created, shaped and formed by human meaning and discourse.

In her work on modern-day hysterias, Showalter notes that for 'metaphorical' illnesses to receive a diagnosis 'at least three ingredients [are required]: physician enthusiasts and theorists; unhappy, vulnerable patients; and supportive cultural environments' (1997, p 17). In the case of stress all three are in place. Doctors are increasingly likely to diagnose stress, and the enthusiasts and theorists take every opportunity to warn us of its pernicious effects. Unhappy and vulnerable patients, in this case social care staff, are being encouraged to interpret their difficulties through a psychological prism, and vulnerability is assumed even when people are coping with the rigours and demands of work and life. The shift in the cultural environment towards one that accepts the stress and therapeutic discourse is apparent, with employers, unions, legislators and the judiciary accepting its validity. For Showalter, hysteria is a mimetic disorder, in that people mimic socially acceptable ways of exhibiting distress. The social acceptability of the current discourse helps shape our understanding of the pressures we face in our daily lives.

Showalter undoubtedly has a point, though again the impact of social and political change has influenced the way we view ourselves, our problems and potential solutions. The discourse of stress did not emerge from nowhere, nor was it the result of remarkable scientific or biological breakthroughs. While there are always complex dynamics at work in the creation of any social phenomenon, the demise of collective working-class organisations, of which the trade unions played a major part, is instructive in detailing the rise of the discourse of stress.

In a detailed analysis of the rise of work stress, Wainwright and Calnan note the significance of the defeat of the miners' strike of 1984–85, and the symbolism of therapy replacing militancy:

> At the beginning of the dispute the miners were confident of winning: placards and badges made assertive militant demands: 'Coal not dole', 'Victory to the miners'. But by the time of their eventual defeat the mood and the slogans had changed: 'Dig deep for the miners', 'Don't let them starve'. Rather than the image of the self-confident, politically conscious rank and file militant, the striking miners had become victims and charity cases. (Wainwright and Calnan, 2002, p 140)

The call for trade unions to take the issue of workplace stress and its causes seriously had been made before (McDonald and Doyle, 1981). However, as the miners' and other defeats brought into question trade unions' traditional roles and tactics they began to focus more on representing the individual rather than the collective worker. The issue of Health and Safety at Work (HSW) helped bridge individual workers' concerns and the collective interests of the workforce. Who, after all, wants to work in an unsafe working environment? Nevertheless, as Wainwright and Calnan point out, the price of this was the acceptance of a therapeutic discourse, where for 'traditional problems at work to become "legitimate" HSW issues they must be transformed into "causes" of physical or mental harm to the worker. The concept of "stress" is essential to this transformation. Thus, oppressive management becomes "bullying" or "harassment", exploitation must become "excessive demands" or "unreasonable pressure"' (2002, p 143).

A good example of this is given in an article on bullying in social work (Kenny, 2007). One worker, whose workload has increased by 50% and who is struggling to cope, does not see the problem as one of exploitation or oppressive management but one of bullying, which resulted in stress and led her to take her local authority to court. She received an out-of-court settlement. The irony is that the decision to take on the sick role was, according to this worker, rather than seen as a sign of weakness, a way 'to take control of my life and my reputation'. The fact that she describes herself as 'left-wing and an active trade unionist' makes it doubly ironic (Kenny, 2007, p 17).

As we have seen, fellow workers are increasingly presented as hazardous agents, not mutually supportive allies. An example of this process can be seen in Manchester Metropolitan University's *Guide to managing stress* (Gregson and Looker, 2004). If your pay, or pay rise, is insufficient to maintain or improve your quality of life, leaving little disposable income, the answer is not to organise with your fellow workers to fight for improved pay but to 'save 5p coins for an end of the month extra treat' (Gregson and Looker, 2004, p 11). After all, why organise with your colleagues when they are being presented as sources of so much bullying and harassment, as the 'fangs of the sabre-tooth tiger' (Gregson and Looker, 2004, p 2).

The construction of the vulnerable, sick worker surrounded on all sides by malevolent forces brings with it new work relationships. For example, the solution to work problems increasingly lies with your doctor by way of a diagnosis of stress and a prescription of rest. As Patmore (2006) notes, workers are being portrayed as too sick to strike, with unions, rather than encouraging them to take industrial action, supporting them to take industrial *inaction*. For Patmore, this 'best to rest' ethos can be viewed as the new opium of the masses.

Such work sheds some light on the tendency described earlier, whereby material issues such as resources are given less priority than other 'unhealthy' factors said to induce stress. It would be wrong to assume that workers are passive recipients of the stress discourse and concomitant sick role; negotiation and resistance to it does take place, for example, many people refuse to accept, or act according to, their doctor's advice (Wainwright and Calnan, 2002). Nevertheless, there are powerful cultural influences at work that can embed themselves in the psyche. As Parker notes, 'a subjectivity is produced in discourse as the self is subjected to discourse' (1989, p 64), and the lack of alternative solutions make us more amenable to therapeutic explanations for our problems. This has consequences for all workers, but an additional, more problematic one for social workers. While all who identify themselves as 'work stress' victims necessarily relinquish agency and adopt the sick role to a greater or lesser extent, the social worker also runs the risk of turning their subjective feeling of vulnerability against those whom they are meant to help, their clientele, who may get constructed as the cause of their distress and seen as pathogenic agents.

Challenging stress

Rather than being seen as an 'illness' in the traditional sense, 'stress' needs to be seen as a historical development carried in discourse and shaped by political, cultural and social factors. Once again, we can see links between the construction of stress and factors discussed earlier.

The 'psy-complex' has developed, with the professions and theories of counselling, psychology, psychotherapy, psychoanalysis and psychiatry expanding, not only within their specialisms, but more importantly into wider societal discourse. Increasingly, ever more aspects of human interaction are seen as problematic, of being hazardous to our health and interpreted through a psychological prism. Within professional discourse there is a tendency to view the subject as a vulnerable one, unable to cope not only with the rigours of life but with what were in the past seen as more mundane, if unpleasant, aspects of social existence.

In a period where the 'truths' of the past have been eroded, where people are said to be 'disembedded' from tradition and community relations (Giddens, 1991), people are trying to locate themselves and their problems in alternative ways. Where once social class explanations for alienation and workplace conflict would have been common, the demise of class politics and the changing role of trade unions have been pivotal in the emergence of the phenomenon of work stress. This shift from the material to the psychological can be seen in the research on stress in social work, in which workers identified lack of resources as causing them most stress. However, rather than a show of collective strength to argue or fight for improved resources, as a new health and safety problem the solution is more likely to be seen as requiring individual therapeutic help.

Locating these changes in a time of pessimism for social progress suggests that the solution lies not in the realm of the individual psyche, but in the world outside our heads. The vulnerability of and threat to the psychological health of the workforce is exaggerated by government policy makers and social theorists alike, and interventions that demonise 'violent' clients downplay the fact that the most difficult aspect of the work is dealing with the material (and psychological) problems faced by those who need social services' help.

It could be argued that one course of action would be for social workers to take umbrage at their portrayal as weak and vulnerable individuals, unable to cope without expert intervention or protection. Insisting that government at a national and local level focus on social problems such as affordable child care, housing and employment would have more impact on the quality of life of their clientele, a change that would also make their work easier and more rewarding. To do so would require a challenge to the encroachment of measures that pathologise individual and social problems, and of methodologies that seek to reinterpret everyday interactions as health hazards requiring professional intervention, in the process trivialising the relatively rare occasions when the demands of social work can indeed be hazardous.

SEVEN

From at risk to a risk: regulating social work

Introduction

This chapter discusses the drive towards registration of the social care workforce, detailing the rationale for, and implications of, such measures. These developments should not be seen in isolation; rather they are part of the process discussed in preceding chapters, in which the discourse of risk, vulnerability and abuse is widespread. Chapter Five looked at how this concern with risk minimisation influences both policy and practice in relation to statutory mental health work. Social workers were shown here to be charged with the assessment of risk. Chapter Six further developed this by showing how social workers themselves are presented as being at risk, whether from service users, colleagues or the pressures of work itself. Here, we discuss a relatively recent development within social work: the setting up of the General Social Care Council (GSCC) and the new requirements it demands of social workers. In this, not only do we see increased levels of regulation placed on social workers, but also see a shift of focus whereby social workers are presented as being a risk to those in their care.

The 2000 Care Standards Act (CSA) proposed major changes in the regulation and provision of social work practice and training, many of which are now in place or about to be established. The CSA required the setting up of a 'body corporate to be known as General Social Care Council' (section 54(1)), which was charged with implementing the requirements of the Act. This was part of the agenda set out by New Labour in 1998 in *Modernising social services*, which aimed to 'improve the protection of vulnerable people' (DH, 1998b, p 9).

It is the duty of the GSCC to promote:

- high standards of conduct and practice among social care workers; and
- high standards in training. (section 2)

Section 56 places a duty on the GSCC to maintain a register of social workers and social care workers, while section 62 requires it to prepare and from time to time publish codes of practice laying down 'standards of conduct and practice expected of social care workers'. In 2002 the GSCC published the national *Codes of practice for social care workers and employers*, and 1 April 2003 saw the introduction of the social care register.

The criteria for registration are based on section 58 of the CSA, which requires the GSCC to be satisfied that the applicant:

• is of good character [declaring criminal convictions and providing an employer endorsement];
• is physically and mentally fit to perform the whole or part of the work [of a social worker or social care worker];
• has successfully completed an approved social work course [for those wishing to be social workers]; and
• has read, understood and agreed to comply with the codes of practice for social care workers.

The drive for registration

Professional registration within social work is not particularly new. Almoners (hospital-based or medical social workers) developed professional bodies and registration from 1903, setting up training and registration of those who qualified from its training school. Similarly, the Association of Psychiatric Social Workers, which was established in 1930, had set up a process of registration for its graduates by 1961 (Malherbe, 1980). Malherbe notes how attempts to adopt a unified registration scheme of qualified workers proved unworkable, partly because of the disparity of organisational groupings, but also because of the large numbers of unqualified workers in the social care field. After the formation of the British Association of Social Workers in 1970, attempts at restricting membership to those with the appropriate qualifications proved unsuccessful, this time as a result of charges from some radicals that such a move was elitist (Payne, 2002).

The GSCC's predecessor, the Central Council for Education and Training in Social Work (CCETSW), also held a register of those who had completed one of its approved social work courses. So in this sense the setting up of a register is nothing new. What is different is that those wishing to be put on the register have to apply formally for registration and pay a fee, undergo an enhanced criminal records bureau check (which also details any cautions and any other information that a chief constable deems appropriate, such as acquittals, surveillance or suspicion), complete a health questionnaire to the satisfaction of the GSCC, and also abide by the code of conduct. The GSCC can remove people from the register if they have reason to do so (examples could include professional misconduct, criminal activity or failure to comply with the code of conduct). With 'protection of title' in force from 1 April 2005, only those on the register can call themselves 'social workers'. This means that for the first time the profession's governing body has the power to block or remove someone's professional status and to stop them working as a social worker.

This drive to registration within social work follows similar moves within the professions of psychotherapy and counselling. Improving the public perception of these disciplines and protecting the public from rogue practitioners was also put forward as the primary objective of statutory control (House, 1997).

There is some ambiguity in the regulatory approach to social work enacted by the New Labour government since its election in 1997. Payne (2005) sees the extension of professional training from two to three years and the registration scheme as positive for the profession, in that these developments comply with European Union regulations for the recognition of a profession. These new arrangements can therefore be seen as strengthening the professional status of social workers. However, as he notes, it has also extended the regulatory process to a wider group of people than qualified social workers, to include all '"care workers", from whom social workers are not clearly differentiated. For example, all workers must comply with a "code of conduct" presented in terms of general accountability, effectiveness and probity, rather than the traditional "codes of ethics" based on professional values' (Payne, 2005, p 196).

In addition, Payne notes how the Labour government has continued with the process of managerialism and accountability initiated by the previous Conservative administration, measures that have contributed to a loss of professional autonomy for social workers. It could be added that the nature of the prescribed curriculum for the new social work degree also undermines professional autonomy. Nevertheless, there is a more significant influence on the drive for registration today: the perception that danger and abuse are omnipresent, and that therefore ever more levels of control are required to protect us from each other.

Social workers were encouraged to apply for registration by 1 December 2004, in order for all applicants to be checked and fully registered by the legal deadline of 1 April 2005. However, six weeks before the December date a report in *Community Care* magazine claimed that in half of English councils only 10% of social workers had applied for registration (*Community Care*, 21 October 2004), giving concern about repercussions for service provision if frontline workers were not registered by the legal deadline. Despite the slow initial take up, the number of registrants is now over 90,000, prompting GSCC chief executive Lynne Berry to claim that such a figure 'shows that social workers and student social workers are embracing their professional status' (GSCC media release, 1 February 2007). Given that they effectively have no choice if they wish to gain or remain in employment it may be an exaggeration to say registration is being embraced, but it is the case that there has been relatively little criticism of the developments.

The GSCC expects social care workers to abide by the code of practice and may take action against those who fail to do so. The code 'is a list of statements that describe the standards of professional conduct and practice required of social care workers as they go about their daily business' (GSCC, 2002, p 2). Those who fail to comply face the possibility of being de-registered as a social worker.

The code stipulates that social care workers must:

1. protect the rights and promote the interests of service users and carers;
2. strive to establish and maintain the trust and confidence of service users and carers;
3. promote the independence of service users while protecting them as far as possible from danger or harm;
4. respect the rights of service users while seeking to ensure that their behaviour does not harm themselves or other people;
5. uphold public trust and confidence in social care services; and
6. be accountable for the quality of their work and take responsibility for maintaining and improving their knowledge and skills (GSCC, 2002).

Within each broad category are included criteria expanding on the GSCC's requirements of social care workers. For example, 3.6 instructs the social worker to abide by their employer's health and safety regulations 'including those related to substance abuse', while 3.2 states that the social worker must 'challenge and report ... discriminatory or exploitative behaviour'. Given the previous discussion in Chapter Three around anti-oppressive practice and work with asylum seekers, which found widespread discrimination in the way social services treat them, one does not need to be a natural cynic to form the opinion that 3.6 will be enforced more vigorously than will 3.2. It is hard to imagine the GSCC de-registering social services departments for discriminating against asylum seekers, but easy to imagine individual workers being targeted for failure to comply with their employer's regulations.

In addition to the social care register and codes of practice, the Protection of Vulnerable Adults (POVA) scheme was launched in July 2004. POVA is laid down by section 80 of the CSA and is a system whereby 'known abusers' of vulnerable adults will have their names put on a register. Care providers in England and Wales will have a statutory duty to consult the register whenever they employ someone whose work involves care duties for those considered vulnerable. Similar registers, POCA (the Protection of Children Act list) and List 99 (run by the Department for Children, Schools and Families) exist to prevent unsuitable people gaining employment working within social care or education establishments respectively.

POVA, as laid down by section 80 of the CSA, requires care agencies to refer a worker to the list if they have been suspended, sacked or moved to a non-care role because of evidence or suspicion that they have harmed a service user or placed them in danger. In addition, care agencies must consult POVA before employing a care worker, and cannot employ anyone whose name appears on the list. It is a criminal offence, punishable by up to five years in prison, for someone whose name appears on the list to seek employment in a care position.

The stated aim of these developments is to protect the public and increase their confidence in social workers, and simultaneously improve the quality of care offered by social workers. Reports have shown low public support for social workers in recent years. For example, in one study, only 40% of respondents thought that social workers played a very important role in society – in contrast to the police, teachers and nurses, who all got over 80%, and doctors, who got 96% (NOP, 2003, cited on GSCC website, www.gscc.org.uk). It will be a key role of the GSCC to 'promote awareness of and respect for the social care workforce', and, according to then UK health minister Jacqui Smith, 'the social care register will be a key part of that work' (see GSCC website). This is not an easy task when, in one UK *Guardian* columnist's view, the public view social workers as 'politically correct dipsticks' (Batty, 2002). According to the GSCC:

> The register is being introduced to support high standards
> of care and public protection in the social care workforce,

through checking of fitness to practice, character and relevant training. It will promote public confidence in the training and credentials of social workers, whilst creating a mechanism to remove those found to be unsuitable. (GSCC, 2003b, p 2)

In addition, POVA will, according to the Department of Health, be a 'key tool' in preventing the abuse of vulnerable adults. Community care minister, Stephen Ladyman, claims that, 'Together with existing Criminal Records Bureau disclosures, references and other good pre-employment practices, the POVA scheme will mean that those intent on harming vulnerable adults will find it extremely difficult to find jobs in care homes and domiciliary care settings' (*Guardian*, 26 July 2004).

The chief executive of the Registered Nursing Home Association sees the introduction of POVA as 'an essential additional safeguard for nursing home owners to help them to prevent anybody who poses a risk to our patients being employed in their homes' (*Guardian*, 26 July 2004). In addition, it is now a requirement of professional social work education courses to ensure student social workers are subject to an enhanced criminal records check. Given the widespread scope of these measures it is worth considering the responses that they have generated. As we will see, it appears that by using the rhetoric of public protection any opposition can be successfully muted.

Responding to regulation

Considering that the social care register, codes of practice and POVA scheme amount to an unprecedented increase in the regulation of the workforce, the measures have attracted very little criticism. Indeed, one study carried out by MORI in 2002 on behalf of the GSCC found that 87% of social workers were in favour of the social care register (DH, 2001c). Where there is criticism it is not against the proposals per se, but that they are not wide-ranging enough, or over who should pay the yearly registration fee. Help the Aged, the older people's charity, claims that POVA is flawed because it does not cover NHS or day care staff. The charity's health and social care policy officer Rachael Childs called for 'a rapid introduction of the POVA register for all health and social care teams together with full criminal records checks on care workers' (*Guardian*, 26 July 2004).

In Britain, the public service union Unison advised its members against registering until it resolved its dispute with the employers over who would fund the cost of registration (*Community Care*, 22

July 2004). It has been left to its equivalent in Northern Ireland, the Northern Ireland Public Service Alliance (NIPSA), to voice a more detailed objection to registration. According to NIPSA's assistant general secretary Kevin McCabe, 'One of the issues we are concerned about is the balance of proof. If a complaint is made against a nurse it must be proved beyond all reasonable doubt. But a social worker's guilt must be judged against the much lesser standard of balance of probabilities' (*Community Care*, 30 April 2004). Nevertheless, the British Association of Social Workers (BASW) has announced its commitment to the 'balance of probabilities' rather than the more stringent 'beyond reasonable doubt' threshold.

A closer look at *Community Care*'s own research on the GSCC and registration revealed some ambiguity. In terms of raising standards, while 70% of respondents thought that registration would achieve this, 54% thought it would take a long time, indicating that registration per se is insufficient to raise standards. Similar results were found in relation to raising the profile and status of social care staff. Of particular interest is the response to the question, 'Which groups should you exclude from the registration requirement?'. Forty-seven per cent thought unskilled/ inexperienced staff without qualifications should be excluded from the requirement to register; one-third thought professionally qualified workers (eg social workers) should be exempt, while only 2% thought that those with no client contact should be exempt from registration (www.communitycare.co.uk, 31 March 2004).

Given that a stated aim of registration is to protect the vulnerable, it is strange that those with most contact with the vulnerable (unskilled/ inexperienced staff) are viewed as requiring registration to a lesser extent than those with less contact (qualified workers), while those with no, or minimal, contact (management, development officers etc) are seen as the group most in need of registration. The profession may be more interested in protection of title than protection of the public.

While the GSCC can claim that 87% of social workers are in favour of the social care register, the *Community Care* survey found that 65% of respondents did not have confidence that the registration scheme would prevent unsuitable people (eg those dismissed for gross misconduct) from working. The same percentage were also concerned that the register could be misused or misadministered, and as a result prevent good people from getting jobs, while 66% had reservations about the GSCC having the power to strike people off the register (www.communitycare.co.uk, 31 March 2004).

The above objections notwithstanding, there is little opposition to the idea that increased regulation is warranted and necessary. However, any measure that can at a stroke regulate a substantial number of the workforce deserves a more critical appraisal.

Registering distrust

Public suspicion of social workers is not particularly new (Popplestone, 1971; Bryant, 1973). In the 1980s and 1990s, there were some high-profile cases involving children and social services. After tragic failures to protect children such as Jasmine Beckford and Kimberley Carlisle, both of whom were killed by their carers, social workers were accused of not intervening quickly enough. By contrast, when, in a period of five months, social workers removed 85 children from their parents in Cleveland, on suspicion that the children were being sexually abused, they were accused of being over-zealous and failing to consider the rights of parents (Parton, 1989).

The case of eight-year-old Victoria Climbie, who was murdered by her aunt and her aunt's boyfriend in 2000, just six months after being discharged back to their care following hospital treatment for severe scalding, shows that the tensions involved in social work between care and control are still evident today. In such tragic and emotive cases it is not surprising that answers are demanded and action to remedy the mistakes implemented. Nevertheless, it is worth asking whether such plans will prove beneficial or could make the problem worse. For example, the tension between care and control will not be easily resolved by the setting up of a register. None of the terrible cases cited above were the result of criminal or unofficial social workers.

In fact, it could be argued that the expansion of criminal records checks is unlikely to make much impact at all. Frontline workers involved in such cases are already subject to enhanced criminal records checks, and the extension of such checks is likely to have little effect on reducing the number of tragedies or instances of malpractice – it is the frontline workers who will make the ultimate decision over removal of a child. And the 'new' codes of conduct for social care work are not particularly new; the GSCC even admitted that they are merely a nationalisation of the kind of models of good practice that already exists in most localities (GSCC, 2002).

In relation to offending behaviour, there have been measures that have made it harder for those with criminal convictions to enter social work, and which have undermined the 'rehabilitative ideal' contained in the 1974 Rehabilitation of Offenders Act. Instructions issued by CCETSW in 1989 required social work training providers to consider any convictions that an applicant may possess and judge their suitability for the course. This initially took the form of asking prospective students to sign a self-disclosure form stating whether or not they had any criminal convictions (CCETSW, 1989b).

The disclosure of convictions does not automatically preclude students from embarking on social work training. It is expected that issues such as the nature of the offence, the time lapsed since it was committed and any mitigating circumstances be taken into consideration when making a decision on suitability. This procedure was, and is, seen as having two benefits. For the service user it offers protection from those who may harm or abuse them, and for the student it stops them wasting two (now three) years of study only to find that their convictions preclude them from taking up a career as a qualified social worker.

Research has shown that the 1989 CCETSW requirement and the potential for formal police checks to be made by placement providers had an effect in dissuading offenders from applying for social work training (Perry, 2004). Perry also found that the possession of criminal convictions is not a reliable guide to assessing criminal behaviour. It reports only those who were charged and subsequently convicted, which leaves those who did not get caught free to undertake a career in social work. For example, when asking students on a social work course to disclose 'offending behaviour' anonymously, not convictions, a significant percentage admitted to a range of incidents, including theft, fraud, violence/assault and sex-related offences. These findings were similar to an earlier study undertaken on probation officers (McGuire and Priestly, 1985). Given that the abuse of vulnerable people by social workers is extremely rare, it would appear that past misdemeanours do not make the social worker a threat to public safety. Similarly, the expansion of criminal records checks seems to be a bureaucratic response to a perceived ubiquitous threat with little evidence that they improve public safety.

Acknowledging that no formal records are available to analyse how decisions are made with regard to the suitability for training of those students who do disclose criminal convictions, Perry argues from his experience that:

> policy debates at training partnership meetings suggest that offender rehabilitation has not been the prime consideration. If anything, the fear of crime – coming from the public generally, the parents of children or vulnerable service users themselves – was likely to be as influential, if not more so, than predictions about the offending behaviour

of particular individuals or ambitions about rehabilitation.
(Perry, 2004, p 999)

It is also not clear just what is regarded as an acceptable level of physical or mental fitness for social workers, or indeed how such a stipulation can be squared with the requirements of the 1995 Disability Discrimination Act and related legislation. Without explicitly saying so, it is likely that the GSCC is here predominantly concerned with mental rather than physical health, the gaze of the GSCC extending to inside the social worker's mind. However, suffering from chronic or episodic acute episodes of mental distress does not necessarily prevent someone from being a good, professional social worker. Indeed, in some settings, for example, within the mental health service, such experience could be deemed an asset. There is a rather distasteful paradox here in that, while social work commits itself to user involvement in the provision of training, consultancy and service provision, at the same time it is using a medical framework with which to preclude such users from actually joining the profession. Reasonable adjustments and a caring response rather than a bureaucratic, medically framed reaction would be more fitting with the values of social work. The Disability Rights Commission has come out against the imposition of such health checks, arguing that there is no correlation between health status and suitability to practice (DRC, 2007). The GSCC has taken this on board and has recently asked the government to remove health check requirement from the 2000 Care Standards Act (GSCC, 2008, www.gscc.org.uk).

Seen in this light, it is possible to suggest that the social care register and code of conduct are more like the enforcement of a new moral code, fuelled by anxiety, rather than something that will improve either social workers' practice or their public image. The register and the code will, however, allow the authorities far greater intrusion into social workers' lives.

Increasing public confidence in social workers will take a lot more than codes, registers and regulations. As we have seen, many within the social work profession have played a part in cultivating a sense of fear and distrust in society, blurring the definitions of abuse to render the term almost meaningless, and portraying everyone as vulnerable. In fact, the tendency to class all those over 18 years of age and who use community care services as 'vulnerable' is a very recent development. The 1948 National Assistance Act differentiated people into specific client groups, related to 'mental disorder', age or illness. It was not until children's services were clearly demarcated that adult services also became recognised as distinct services in their own right

(Baldwin, 2000). Soon, though, as Slater notes, 'In gaining explicit currency, however, the term "adult" was increasingly coupled with the attribute "vulnerable". Indeed, under the auspices of Part VII of the Care Standards Act 2000, any adult user of residential or domiciliary care or prescribed medical services expressly became a "vulnerable adult"' (2004, p 652).

There was now a commitment to 'prevent and root out the abuse and neglect of vulnerable people' (DH, 1998b, p 64). The initial concern was with preventing abuse by professionals/services upon service users. This was soon extended to include 'personal and family relations within domiciliary locations', in the Orwellian-sounding policy document *No secrets* (DH, 2000d, p 11). Under the remit of 'protection', once again the boundary of the public/private, personal/political was further undermined. This intention to 'prevent and root out' cases of abuse, with its emphasis on prevention, 'considers positive guarantees of human rights rather than a more negative stance of responding to selected violations after the event' (Brammer, 2001, p 44).

The increasing trend to view us all as weak and vulnerable not only heightens anxiety but portrays us all as either abusers or abused. It should perhaps then be no surprise that the end result is a suspicion of both the public and professionals, a sense that danger and abuse are around every corner. There is a possibility here that the more the social work profession highlights abuse, danger and vulnerability as being everywhere, the lower people's confidence in social workers will get. After all, a profession that sees its role as preventing abuse is admitting its own failure when it portrays things as always getting worse. Perhaps one way to improve the image and effectiveness of the social care profession would be for social work policy makers to have faith in the ability of the vast majority of the population to cope without them, and to stop viewing everyone as a potential abuser. After all, if social workers do not trust the public or themselves, why should the public trust them?

The 24/7 social worker

It is clear from the code of practice that being a social care worker is not seen as a 9–5 job, where there is a clear separation of work/home/private life. Indeed, the criteria gives both employers and the GSCC, via the registration process, unprecedented regulation over the workforce, whether in the office, pub or at home. For example, workers must not 'Behave in a way, in work *or outside work*, which would call into question [their] suitability to work in social care services' (GSCC, 2002, 5.8, emphasis added).

Here, we can see the extension of public scrutiny into the private and personal life of the social worker. Complying with the employer's policies on substance abuse within the working day – for example not going to the pub for a drink at lunchtime, or not smoking cannabis at a tea-break – may be relatively uncontroversial, but what if that extends to outside office hours? More worrying, though, is the unspecified behaviours that must comply with social care service requirements. Such a specification clearly extends the employer's control into areas hitherto considered outside their remit.

Such a stipulation could include any subsequent criminal conviction that occurs while the social worker is in post, and which would call into question their suitability for the position. Again, such a situation will probably raise relatively little concern, although even non-criminal offences such as driving while over the alcohol limit have seen the worker brought before the GSCC conduct committee (www.gscc.org. uk, GSCC media release, 8 March 2007). This provision, in principle, also provides the authorities with unprecedented powers to regulate and decide on many more aspects of non-work life. Political and religious beliefs can also be covered by such a stipulation, implicitly giving employers, in many cases the local authority, the right to decide what are 'correct' and 'appropriate' political or religious affiliations and beliefs. The GSCC is, after all, a body set up by Parliament, which, by use of the discourse of vulnerability and abuse, will be able to police the behaviour and affiliations of a large number of the social care workforce.

By May 2006 more than 400 social workers had been referred to the GSCC for alleged misconduct; 161 of them were assessed as requiring no further action. However, 50 had been referred to the 'preliminary proceedings committee' and 191 were still being investigated (Carson, 2006). A look on the conduct hearings section of its website (www. gscc.org.uk) reveals a wide-ranging catalogue of misconduct that the GSCC sees as within its remit to put forward to a full conduct hearing. This includes cases where social workers have engaged in sexual or 'inappropriate' contact with clients, of social workers convicted of drink driving, of failing to disclose criminal convictions, of sending and receiving emails of an 'offensive and discriminatory' nature, and a case where a worker had physically restrained a service user.

In deciding these cases, the conduct committee, whose make up is independent of the GSCC, has used the full range of its powers: immediate removal of the worker from the social care register, suspension for a limited period and admonishment. The admonishment would be detailed next to the worker's record for a specified period of time. There are certainly cases here where few people would disagree that the worker concerned should not be allowed to work with vulnerable people. However, it is less clear that such procedures protect the public or warrant the extension of surveillance and control over a substantial number of the workforce. For example, perhaps one of the most severe cases involved a social worker who had sex with a depressed woman who had been referred to him for assessment. He subsequently lost his job, was jailed and then suspended from the social care register. If there has to be a social care register then this man should certainly not be on it. Nevertheless, such a course of action will have no bearing on future public safety; the criminal conviction alone would be enough to prevent him from working in such a setting again.

The social care register and the GSCC's monopoly over who should and should not be on it is also problematic in a practical sense. Social work is a very diverse field, with various client groups and settings in which social workers operate. In instances of criminal convictions and/or health issues, individual employers are best placed to decide whether or not the applicant or worker should be offered employment or should remain in post. Criminal convictions could be viewed differently depending on the nature of the post. Drug convictions may be seen more positively in a drug setting, being seen as giving the worker insight into the current problems of the client group. Similarly with health issues, someone with past or present mental health problems may be seen to have something to offer as a result of that experience. A monolithic body such as the GSCC is not representative of the diversity of services or settings in which social workers are employed today.

The focus on the behaviour of individual workers not only detracts from the more structural problems facing social services provision, it increasingly undermines any notion of a public/private divide and contains within it a moral framework by which we are all to be judged. For example, the first case to go before the GSCC's conduct committee concerned a female social worker who had advertised herself as an escort. She was suspended from the register for two years. Although this decision was upheld when her appeal to the Care Standards Tribunal was rejected, the case contains some worrying elements. The tribunal concluded that 'misconduct is about lack of integrity and how an individual is *perceived by others*' (CST, 2006, p 3, emphasis added). The tribunal also interchangeably uses the terms 'escort' and 'prostitution' when in fact the former is a legal activity, soliciting for the latter illegal. It also feels able to assert that the woman had sexual intercourse with a man she met through the escort agency by interpreting an email exchange as containing sexual innuendo implying that she did.

This combination of moral policing and decisions based on the perception of others raises many issues, not least the fact that what is considered appropriate and inappropriate behaviour can change over time. In the 1970s homosexuality was viewed as an immoral activity by many people, and while the social work profession likes to portray itself as at the forefront of combating oppression, the *British Journal of Social Work*, arguably its most prestigious journal, published an article at this time advocating the use of aversion therapy with gay men, in order, no doubt, to avert them from such 'immoral' behaviour (Graham, 1971). If the GSCC had been in existence in the early 1970s, then people indulging in homosexual activity may have been deemed to be committing misconduct. Given the tabloid press hostility towards homosexuals at that time such a decision could have been justified on the basis of how the gay or lesbian worker was likely to be perceived by others.

In the wake of the above case there was a discussion in *Community Care* magazine about what other 'private' behaviour could be deemed as constituting misconduct. So, while excessive drinking is considered problematic, regular attendance at a lap-dancing club is seen as beyond the pale (although one visit out of curiosity or for a leaving-do is considered okay) (Leason, 2006). There is a dangerous trajectory to this debate. For example, as I point out elsewhere, why stop there? What about regular attendance at Roy 'Chubby' Brown gigs, or previously attending the late Bernard Manning's gigs, neither comedian being known for upholding social work values? Would it be inappropriate to attend a public gig, but okay to watch their videos in private at home? Then again, what about buying rap records that contain sexist or homophobic lyrics (McLaughlin, 2007)?

Despite such tensions, the GSCC does not appear to have any qualms about increasing the focus on such behaviour. A recent newspaper advertisement asks the question 'How many discriminatory jokes are too many?' before telling us that 'For social workers the answer's one' and that making such jokes 'is a serious breach of the Code of Conduct' (*Guardian*, Society 2, 27 June 2007). We are not informed just who decides what is considered a discriminatory joke, but the implication is that the GSCC will not only watch what we do but also police what we say.

In another case in which the social worker appealed to the Care Standards Tribunal, the tribunal while dismissing the appeal pointed out its view that the GSCC had put 'the most sinister interpretation on untested evidence', failing to take into account the possibility of misunderstandings caused by cultural and language difficulties (CST, 2007). While the tribunal is correct to point this out, the GSCC in many ways is merely doing what it is supposed to do: view us all through suspicious eyes, as potentially deviant subjects who require constant surveillance.

The need for privacy

The lack of critical reaction against the extension of state authority into workers' lives reveals not only contempt for the notion of the private sphere but also failure to grasp its importance. The need for a place away from public scrutiny is important for our sense of self. This is what Goffman (1959) called the 'backstage' region. The backstage region was a place away from the public gaze, a more private space that allowed the person to act in a less formal, more natural way, as opposed to the public presentation of the self. This arena away from the public gaze was not necessarily the home. For Goffman, such areas were necessary at work as well. He contrasts the informal, sometimes childish and sloppy interaction between workers in the 'privacy' of the office or shopfloor with their behaviour if all such work was completed in front of the customer. This analysis is functional in that he sees the backstage area as one where people can let off steam and be themselves, and therefore it serves a useful social function. Indeed, in his work on total institutions, it was the way asylums eliminated this 'backstage', or private, arena that in part led to the destruction of the patient's former identity; their every move became a matter of medical scrutiny (Goffman, 1961).

Of course the idea that it is possible to separate rigidly the public and private spheres has been well acknowledged. The home, rather than being a safe, private place has been shown to be somewhere in which violence and abuse can take place. According to MacKinnon, 'the legal concept of privacy can and has shielded the place of battery, marital rape, and women's exploited labour' (quoted in Cohen, 1997, p 141). This feminist analysis has been most influential in social work, and in highlighting the political nature of such issues they were also held to be legitimate sites of political intervention (Dominelli, 2002).

It is certainly correct that there is no clear-cut, rigid disjuncture between the political and the personal, the public and private. Attempts to define it legally are always problematic. Even sex, which most people may regard as a private matter, usually involves at least one other person, and for some feminists (eg Dworkin, 1981), including social work academics (eg Dominelli, 2002), the moment we are in the realm of interpersonal relations we enter the public, political sphere. Nevertheless, there are problems with this collapse of any distinction between the terms.

In attempting to transcend this amorphous dichotomy, Wolfe (1997) proposes a 'trichotomy' comprising the 'private', the 'public' and the 'publics'. These *publics* operate in what we more commonly refer to as 'civil society', the sphere of self-generating communities and networks outside the state. However, increasingly, through partnership with the voluntary sector, the state has changed the nature of these *publics*. Writers such as Giddens (2000) see the process of partnership as being indicative of a move towards governance and democratisation. This misses the way that increased state intervention has limited the extent to which such organisations can develop and grow organically. Instead they become contrived spaces in which governmental control is increased. As Hodgson notes:

> While the rhetoric is one of collaboration, the government has in fact continued its 'command and control'... style of governing through 'criteria setting', auditing and centrally-imposed initiatives. Viewed in this light, manufactured civil society can be viewed as a means of controlling what happens within the community and civil society more broadly. Rather than a redistribution of power and influence, what we may be witnessing is the extension of state power via a range of social actors. (Hodgson, 2004, p 157)

The extension of the state/*public* into civil society/*publics* represents a manufactured domain with which social conformity can be imposed, and these social actors include social workers. For example, as discussed earlier the concept of anti-racist and anti-oppressive practice includes an element of increased state control via the imposition of the 'correct' thoughts, words and behaviours. Such developments were, in the main, top-down, a state agency dictating to the people how to behave (Penketh, 2000). In similar vein, governmental values are being imposed on civil society.

As an attempt to keep some form of distinction between personal and interpersonal matters on the one hand, and more public/political matters on the other, Wolfe (1997) is also attempting to limit the scope for state intrusion into ever more aspects of people's lives. Nevertheless, he is too optimistic, in part because his analysis of the reasons for the state's ability to intervene fails to recognise the diminished view of humanity prevalent today. These 'intermediate' groups or *publics*, as he calls them, are increasingly being colonised by a therapeutic, professional discourse that views them with suspicion.

It is not so much that people do not accept the need for some form of privacy, rather that an ever-growing myriad of human interactions are seen as potentially abusive or oppressive. In this sense, even Wolfe's *publics* are viewed with suspicion, and therefore subject to *public* scrutiny and intervention. There is hardly any form of *publics*, if by this we mean interaction with other individuals or institutions, that has not been tainted by accusations of abuse. As noted earlier, familial relations were cast as sites where domestic violence and/or child abuse were prevalent. Similar charges have been made against social work, organisationally due to institutional failings (eg Levy and Kahan, 1991), and individually due to cases where social workers have abused children in their care (eg Warner, 1992). Even the Church has had to admit to the existence of paedophile priests within its ranks, and to its role in covering up some serious cases where such priests had sexually abused children (*Guardian*, 26 October 2005).

In general, there have been two competing viewpoints of the need for social work. The first was a humanitarian one, in which a civilised society protected those who could not care for themselves; the second, from an anti-humanist perspective, argued that people were inherently selfish and uncaring, therefore some form of state provision was necessary to protect the weak from the strong (Payne, 2005). In many respects, the worst aspects of both approaches are evident today. Not only is there a tendency to portray everyone as weak and vulnerable and therefore in need of help and support, but simultaneously they are seen as potentially dangerous and predatory, and therefore in need of supervision and control.

It is this degraded view of humanity, where everyone is now seen as a potential abuser or victim that allows *public* authorities growing scope to monitor the nation's *publics*, and increasingly the private sphere also. The need for welfare provision because of need 'from the cradle to the grave', which contained within it a notion of a caring society, has been replaced by one of suspicion and surveillance. Societal need has been replaced by societal abuse as the focus of state intervention.

Social workers invariably find themselves working at the boundary of the public/private divide. If they intervene too readily they are liable to face accusations of state intrusion and moral policing; if they fail to intervene they stand accused of failing to protect the vulnerable. Increasingly, however, there has been a steady erosion of the concept of the private sphere for society as a whole. This trend also affects social workers as they find their conduct, both in and outside work subject to the scrutiny of the General Social Care Council.

EIGHT

Politics and social work

Introduction

The 'radical social work' movement of the 1970s highlighted the class struggle in British society at the time, and the way in which social work acted in the interests of the ruling class (Bailey and Brake, 1975). In the 1980s, social work embraced other factors such as sexuality, race and gender as areas where oppression occurred, either in association with, or irrespective of, social class (Langan and Lee, 1989). Today, there are also voices calling for social work to awaken from its slumber and recognise areas of current practice that do not fit well with its egalitarian principles. In this chapter I discuss attempts to 're-politicise' social work and suggest that such a call misses a more fundamental issue whereby politics is overly concerned with social work. I conclude by highlighting ways in which to challenge the contemporary consensus.

Social work as politics

In 'Social work and social justice: a manifesto for a new engaged practice', the authors, all leading social work academics, recognise that many people enter social work intending to bring about positive change in people's lives (Jones et al, 2004). They note the increasing managerialism within the social work role, and the way in which the worker–client relationship is increasingly characterised by control and supervision rather than care. 'Technical' fixes such as the new social work degree or the setting up of general social care councils are viewed as insufficient to address the current situation. Social work's degraded status is said to be caused by the fact that those they work with – for example young people, poor families, asylum seekers – are also viewed as degraded by society. New Labour's social welfare reforms mean that in many cases 'social workers are often doing little more than supervising the deterioration of people's lives' (Jones et al, 2004, p 2).

The manifesto's authors view the solution as being for social workers to engage with the 'resources of hope available in the new collective movements for an alternative, and better, world', one based around such values as solidarity and liberty (Jones et al, 2004, p 3). Such a call, while a laudable one, will nevertheless entail a more critical consideration of, and challenge to, social work than is proposed in the manifesto. Indeed, this book has been concerned with how contemporary social work theory and practice has undermined such values as solidarity and liberty. Of course, social work cannot be held solely responsible for a breakdown of societal solidarity. Historical and material changes, in interaction with intellectual attempts to explain such conditions, helped to create a situation in which a degraded view of the human subject became prevalent. Such a view of the human subject can be utilised to curtail rather than extend liberty. It is therefore worth summarising the main points of the book to demonstrate how social work today is detrimental to values such as liberty and solidarity.

Specifically, we saw how the concept of abuse permeated social work in three main ways: social workers as *assessors* of risk, social workers as *at* risk, and social workers as *a* risk. Chapter Five discussed not only the drive towards more coercive mental health legislation, but also the increase in coercion under the present Mental Health Act. Chapter Six showed the way in which our colleagues and intimates are presented as hazardous to our health. The way the discourse of risk and abuse also positions social workers as potential abusers was the focus of Chapter Seven, where, once again, we noted an increase in regulation being justified in the name of public safety. A common theme that emerges is one in which we are not only viewed as malevolent but simultaneously as vulnerable in the face of such omnipresent threats.

As has been discussed in detail, the social work profession has been overtly politicised, especially from the 1970s onwards. However, this politicisation in practice has led to a micropolitical regulatory approach, substituting as it does a focus on interpersonal rather than on social or structural politics. Again, a similar analysis is implicit in Jones et al's (2004) manifesto, which notes how social work has been politicised but is concerned that it has lost any connection with wider political issues and grassroots social movements. This recognition that the current political trajectory is problematic leads to the call being made for collective organisation involving all social workers and service users in an attempt to re-politicise social work and social workers.

Concerned that social work should not be defined by its function for the state but by its value base, social work is exhorted to 'coalesce and organise around a shared vision of what a genuinely anti-oppressive social work might be like' (Jones et al, 2004, p 4). This is, in effect, a contemporary version of the early radical social work movement's call to work both 'in and against the state'. Recognising the importance of user group initiatives such as collective advocacy or organisations such as the Hearing Voices Network – initiatives that did not originate from within social work but from the users themselves – the lesson is for social work to 'engage with, and learn from, these movements in ways that will allow partnerships to form and new knowledge bases and curricula to develop' (Jones et al, 2004, p 2).

How it is in the interests of such groups to form partnerships with social workers is far from clear, and two main problems can be highlighted. First, groups such as the Hearing Voices Network have established themselves without the need for direct social work input, having as part of their remit the exploration of alternative understandings of the causes and solutions to their difficulties. The radical agenda of previous social movements was compromised by their incorporation into the state and its institutions, in turn becoming both increasingly moralistic and authoritarian. If today's groups are making progress outside such agencies then perhaps the best solution, given the lessons of the past, is to leave them to organise themselves. This leads to the second problem: implicit in the call for social workers to make partnerships with such organisations is an assumption that the organisations need the assistance of social workers. However, this is not necessarily the case, and leads me to suggest that the answer may lie, not in re-politicising social work as called for in the new radical manifesto, but on the contrary in depoliticising it.

In the sense that social workers act as gatekeepers to societal resources, ensuring that only those considered eligible can access them, then of course, social work is political and social workers are engaged in political activity as they go about their daily work. The fulfilment of statutory services under community care, mental health or children's legislation is a clear indicator of the political component of the work. The construction of what is defined as a social problem or classed as deviant behaviour will also be influenced by political developments. In addition, social workers are employees and as such will encounter conflict over such things as pay and terms and conditions. Furthermore, some social workers will be more politically active than others, perhaps being involved in mainstream or alternative political organisations or loose affiliations such as the 'anti-capitalist' movement.

While neither of these are contentious in and of themselves, nevertheless the conflation of them can be problematic. If social workers wish to organise to improve their working conditions then that is a matter for them to decide upon. Likewise, if they are politically active outside their workplace, it should be no cause for concern. However, it is a more contentious matter if they use their professional employment in the pursuit of a wider political agenda and to politicise their clientele. What happens, for example, to the social worker whose politics does not fit with the contemporary consensus, or to those in need who may not harbour the same political views as the social worker?

There is no getting away from the fact that social work is, in the main, an activity that takes place within a state agency, with one of its functions being the maintenance of the status quo. If the radical social work movement failed in its entryist agenda for broader social change at a time when there was a politicised labour movement, it is unlikely to be able to use the same strategy successfully today, given the relative weakness of organised labour. In addition, as discussed earlier, it is partly due to previous activists' work that we have a situation whereby social work has become ever more authoritarian and regulatory. The blurring of, indeed for some the failure to acknowledge any distinction between, the public and private, and the concomitant rise of the concept of abuse and the mistrust of people, has played a part in allowing such an encroachment by state authorities into the minutiae of interpersonal relations.

There is also an implicit notion of professional arrogance in the call for social workers to make links with self-help organisations. Certainly, some individuals within such organisations may require social work input at various points and for various periods of time, but it is not so certain that the organisation will gain from collaboration with social workers. It may find itself absorbed and its agenda diluted as it enters the bureaucratic world of social work. It is striking that Jones et al (2004) feel unable to leave self-help groups alone. If they wish to organise with them as part of their wider political identities that is one thing, but to pursue that agenda in the guise of their work is quite another.

A further problem can be identified. The focus on to what extent social work is political misses a more fundamental problem whereby contemporary politics has become reduced to a form of social work. It is in this sense that rather than a re-politicisation of social work, a depoliticisation is suggested.

Politics as social work

Social work, at its most basic, is concerned with the micromanagement of life, working with the vulnerable in order to make small changes to their situation and in the process improve their lives. An understanding of social and psychological influences on subjectivity, interpersonal communication and relationships can help the worker relate to their client and to work with them to identify possible solutions to their current situation. In this sense, an outlook that moves outward from the personal (or political with a small 'p') to the Political (with a capital 'P') can be useful.

Increasingly, though, what we are seeing is the Political gaze looking inward towards the personal, with Politics becoming overtly concerned with the micromanagement of people's personal or interpersonal (with a small 'p') life. This rise of 'third-party intervention' or the 'professionalisation of everyday life' has been well documented (eg Smail, 2001).

This trend looks likely to continue when it is considered that the 10-year period between 1976 and 1986 saw a 66% increase in the number of social workers (Hillyard and Percy-Smith, 1988). Even so, because of concerns that there had been a 50% reduction in applications for social work training between 1997 and 2000 (*Guardian*, 15 February 2000), which would in turn compound a national shortage, the government implemented various measures to recruit and retain more social workers. Stephen Ladyman, speaking in 2003 when he was community care minister, stated the government's intention to invest £21 million into social work education, rising to £81.45 million by 2005/6 (Ladyman, 2003). This included provision for the General Social Care Council (GSCC) to pay the fees and provide around £3,000 per year in bursary payments to all social work students. There was also an advertising campaign to promote the profession. Unsurprisingly, as a consequence of these initiatives the number of applicants for social work training increased (GSCC, 2003a).

Despite this new focus, it is possible to argue that, rather than being indicative of a politicisation of social work, the new initiatives are driven by a desire to focus on the technicalities and practicalities of social work intervention. Addressing the Community Care Live conference in 2002, then health minister Jacqui Smith declared that 'Social work is a very practical job.' Such a declaration can be taken as being the culmination of the trend Dominelli (2002) identified as being a sustained attack on the principles of anti-oppressive practice. Nevertheless, as discussed in Chapter Three, this misses the extent to which anti-oppression has become institutionalised within British society.

In addition, despite the health minister's declaration, there is a strong message contained in her new 'practical' social work, and this message is underpinned by many of the developments highlighted in this book, such as the move to a therapeutic model of understanding and intervening in societal problems, increased intervention in people's lives and a belief that professional help is required in order for people to cope. For example, the Sure Start initiative to help children under the age of five living in deprived areas, which is comprised of multi-agency teams, including social workers, is less concerned with the material effects of poverty than with providing therapeutic 'guidance' around parenting styles. This therapeutic guidance led to measurements of family life being scored around various categories including frequency of swearing and/or smacking and whether the home is disorganised and/or noisy (Melhuish et al, 2004). Social work departments are also actively promoting their 'anti-bullying' strategies within education (eg Cornwall, 2005; Sunderland, 2005). Rather than the government wishing to remove any need for understanding or theoretical explanations for social problems, on the contrary it seems intent on pursuing policies that share a belief in therapeutic interventions and of the need for parenting and coping skills to be taught, not just to a minority of people but to all.

This move, which has been called the 'politics of behaviour' (Field, 2003), encompasses a wide range of agencies and professionals. Schools are increasingly concerned not only with children's education but also with ensuring their lunchboxes contain 'appropriate' healthy snacks (Sandeman, 2006). Housing associations are charged with providing quality accommodation, and also increasingly with the moral policing and surveillance of their tenants' behaviour. In the process, issues of nuisance noise and children gathering get portrayed as due to feckless parents or feral youth rather than inadequate insulation, lack of social amenities and/or poor economic conditions (Flint, 2004). Linked to this is the way housing organisations and youth offending teams are instructed to work in tandem in the implementation and monitoring of Anti-Social Behaviour Orders (www.respect.gov.uk). The government has suggested that health service staff should routinely ask all female patients if they are experiencing domestic violence (Home Office, 2004). Concern over the population's smoking and alcohol consumption also plays a greater role in the policies of both central and local government.

Political ideas and actions are increasingly about the policing of individual behaviour. Politics, even within government, is ever more reduced to the micromanagement of people's lives. It is in this sense that politics has become social work. The desire from the 1970s onwards to politicise those areas of life in which social workers intervened coincided with a general loss of political confidence within left-wing thought for wider social change, which led to a focus on the micropolitical sphere and interpersonal relationships. Of course, while social work may have contributed to the current situation, it is not solely responsible for it. A lack of political vision and ideology affects all political parties today. What social work did do was allow, indeed in many cases demand, governmental intervention into the minutiae of interpersonal relationships. A lack of ideas for social progress in the wider socio-economic sphere can now be articulated as a positive intervention into the behaviour of the community, using local health, social services, housing and a myriad of community groups as its intermediaries. Rather than merely provide social *services*, such organisations increasingly do social *work*.

Without ideological focus, no grand political project, no 'big idea', social work has moved from being an aspect of political life to become one of its defining features. The scope for Politics in an anti-ideological age is reduced. Politics becomes guidance and governance, or where social work is concerned, 'therapeutic governance'. This trend, whereby the relationship between citizen and state institutions is redefined in psychosocial terms is mediated by a professional and managerial class that is, to some extent, governing society (Pupavac, 2001).

This governance is not benign. At its most overt, as discussed in relation to mental health policy and practice, the penalty for refusing to participate with the professionals can be compulsory hospitalisation, or enforced medication in the community. More subtle coercion is in the form of initiatives whereby parenting classes, counselling sessions and anger-management sessions can be 'recommended', with failure to attend or to adopt the 'correct' attitude by the end of the treatment leading to censure and sanction. The fear of physical reprisal is real enough, but there is also fear of the moral and psychological consequences of rejecting the advice, such is the power of the discourse within which such advice operates (Burman et al, 1996).

Bereft of Political ideas, Politics is reduced to the micromanagement of human interaction. Unable to lead or give direction, in a certain respect politicians are ever more reliant on a myriad of professionals, in our case social workers, to give legitimacy to their version of both the causes and cures of social problems.

Politics

In the realm of ideas it is necessary to challenge many of today's dominant beliefs, in particular that we cannot trust one another, or are unable to change anything other than our shoelaces without professional help. Where people do need social services, for whatever reason, then provision can be made. For most of us, for most of the time, the politicisation of social work does little but help foster a climate in which we are patronised or viewed with suspicion and encouraged to view our family, friends and colleagues likewise. This makes it less likely for any form of collectivity, far less the global one hoped for by Jones et al (2004).

It is difficult to forge bonds based on adult solidarity while emphasising that everyone is a potential threat to our well-being. If our intimates, friends and colleagues really are toxic agents hazardous to our health then it makes sense to avoid rather than embrace them. In order to challenge both such an atomising viewpoint and the ongoing erosion of civil liberties it is necessary to show how the rationale behind them is based on exaggerated dangers and flawed methodologies. However, it is problematic to point out such problems in one arena but utilise them in another. The end result is a climate of fear and mistrust. If there is to be any hope of influencing the trajectory of the present debate, a good starting point would be to challenge all the irrational and exaggerated fears of the contemporary age, not just those that suit our particular area of interest. This would allow us to forge bonds based on trust and our potential to overcome both personal and social problems. In doing so we may be able to reverse the breakdown of adult solidarity that will be necessary to challenge the prevailing situation.

A useful start would be for social workers, agencies and campaign groups not to extrapolate from their casework to wider society. This would allow them to concentrate on the cases of abuse and need that they most certainly do encounter on a daily basis, and where necessary to devise strategies for intervention. However, seeing abused children on a daily or weekly basis in your work as, for example, a child protection social worker, does not mean that such cases are indicative of a wider problem in which all children are abused and all adults are potential abusers. Similarly, working each day with women suffering from domestic violence may be traumatic and cause anger and frustration at its causes and effects. Nevertheless, such cases of serious abuse do not make all women victims nor all men abusers, and neither is it helpful to blur boundaries to such an extent that all unpleasant but trivial intimate disputes are categorised as abuse.

Encouraging such a split between the specifics of practice and wider political intervention could also allow us to find a way of traversing the particular and the universal. Individuals in need of help will subjectively interpret those experiences in different ways, and therefore awareness of difference, and of the psychological and social influences on them and their situation, can be utilised to gain an understanding of their circumstances in order to intervene in a positive way. Again, though, extrapolating from such cases to wider society is problematic. Particularism and difference at a wider political level can help isolate and alienate people and communities, with differences becoming entrenched and institutionalised. This, in turn, makes it more difficult to create the conditions that would allow us to unite in our common humanity and agree some universal values. We are, as Jacoby (1999) has pointed out, not as different as we are portrayed; for example, festivals such as Christmas, Chanukah and Kwanzaa can certainly be portrayed as representing cultural differences; they can also be read as representing not differences, but similarities, each with common themes of celebration and coming together, even through they have taken different expressions as a result of their historical and geographical development.

For those concerned with social problems today and wishing to create the conditions for social change, we do need to foster a climate where commonalities can be forged and relationships developed. In this sense, Jones et al's (2004) manifesto is correct. However, it is the contention of this book that politicising social work is not the way to achieve such political ambitions. On the contrary, much social work theory and practice has contributed to the present situation and as such is part of the problem.

Contemporary social work and social theory has helped undermine the old dichotomies around areas such as health and illness, personal and political, public and private. Destabilising these fixed divisions was viewed as progressive by many within social work in allowing individual problems to be seen as social in nature. However, the collapse of any distinction, particularly in a period of diminished subjectivity, also has implications; we can all be seen as sick, politics becomes personal, therapy intrudes into politics.

If this is the case, then there is a need to engage critically with social work's attempts to colonise areas of life in which its input is unhelpful. Similarly, its role in the exaggeration of the concept of abuse, individual vulnerability and the need for third-party professional intervention is not only representative of a diminished view of the human subject, but also perpetuates the problem. There is no need to politicise social work. That was done many years ago. Today the task is to get politics out of social work and therapy out of politics.

References

ADSS (Association of Directors of Social Services) (1982) *The role and tasks of social workers*, London: ADSS.

Alaszewski, A., Alaszewski, H., Ayer, S. and Manthorpe, J. (2000) *Managing risk in community practice*, Edinburgh: Bailliere Tindall.

Alcoff, L. and Gray, L. (1993) 'Survivor discourse: transgression or recuperation?', *SIGNS*, no 18, winter, pp 260-90.

Alibhai-Brown, Y. (1993) 'Social workers need race training not hysteria', *Independent*, 11 August.

Appleby, L. (1997) 'Assessment of suicide risk', *Psychiatric Bulletin*, vol 21, pp 193–4.

Appleby, L., Shaw, J., Kapur, N. and Windfuhr, K. (2006) 'Avoidable deaths: five year report by the national confidential inquiry into suicide and homicide by people with mental illness', www.medicine. manchester.ac.uk/suicideprevention/nci/Useful/avoidable_deaths_full_report.pdf.

Appleyard, B. (1993) 'Why paint so black a picture?', *Independent*, 4 August.

Aptekar, H.H. (1941) *Concepts in social casework*, New York: Columbia University Press.

Arroba, T. and James, K. (1987) *Pressure at work: A survival guide*, London: McGraw-Hill.

Bailey, R. and Brake, M. (eds) (1975) *Radical social work*, London: Edward Arnold.

Baldwin, M. (2000) 'Adults as service users in community care', in M. Davies (ed) *Encyclopaedia of social work*, Oxford: Blackwell.

Balloch, S., McLean, J. and Fisher, M. (1999) *Social services: Working under pressure*, Bristol: The Policy Press.

Balloch, S., Pahl, J. and McLean, J. (1998) 'Working in the social services: job satisfaction, stress and violence', *British Journal of Social Work*, vol 28, pp 329–50.

Banks, S. (1995) *Ethics and values in social work*, London: Macmillan.

Barrett, R.J. (1988) 'Clinical writing and the documentary construction of schizophrenia', *Culture, Medicine and Psychiatry*, vol 12, pp 265–99.

Barrett Report (2006) *Independent inquiry into the care and treatment of John Barrett*, London: NHS London and South West London and St George's Mental Health NHS Trust.

Bass, E. and Davis, L. (1988) *The courage to heal*, London: Cedar.

BASW (British Association of Social Workers) (1977) *The social work task*, Birmingham: BASW.

BASW (2003) 'Asylum briefing', 18 December, www.basw.co.uk.

Batty, D. (2002) 'Unsocial services', *Guardian*, Society, 16 October.

Bean, P. (2001) *Mental disorder and community safety*, Hampshire: Palgrave.

Bebbington, A. and Miles, J. (1989) 'The background of children who enter residential care', *British Journal of Social Work*, vol 19, no 5, pp 349–68.

Beck, U. (1992) *Risk society: Towards a new modernity*, London: Sage.

Beckford Report (1985) *A child in trust*, Wembley: London Borough of Brent.

Bensaid, D. (2002) *A Marx for our times: Adventures and misadventures of a critique*, London: Verso.

Besag, V. (1989) *Bullies and their victims in schools*, Milton Keynes: Open University Press.

Bettleheim, B. (1986) *Freud and man's soul*, London: Flamingo.

Blashfield, R.K. (1996) 'Predicting DSM-V', *Journal of Mental and Nervous Disease*, no 184, pp 4–7.

Bleuler, E. (1911) *Dementia praecox or the group of schizophrenias*, trans. 1950 by J. Zinkin, New York: International Universities Press.

Blewett, J., Lewis, J. and Tunstill, J. (2007) *The changing roles and tasks of social work: A literature informed discussion paper*, London: General Social Care Council.

Blofeld, J., Sallah, D., Sahidharan, S., Stone, R. and Struthers, J. (2003) *Independent inquiry into the death of David Bennett*, Cambridge: Norfolk, Suffolk and Cambridgeshire Strategic Health Authority.

Blom-Cooper, L., Murphy, E. and Hally, H. (1995) *The falling shadow*, Torquay: South Devon Health Care Trust.

Boulton, M.J. and Underwood, K. (1992) 'Bully/victim problems amongst middle school children', *British Journal of Educational Psychology*, vol 62, pp 73–87.

Boyle, M. (1990) *Schizophrenia: A scientific delusion?*, London: Routledge.

Bracken, P. and Thomas, P. (1999) 'Psychiatry and institutional racism', *Open Mind*, no 98, p 14.

Brammer, A. (2001) 'Human Rights Act 1998: implications for adult protection', *Journal of Adult Protection*, vol 3, no 1, pp 43–52.

Bree, M.H. (1970) 'Staying the course', *British Journal of Psychiatric Social Work*, vol 10, no 4, pp 170–7.

Briere, J. and Runtz, M. (1987) 'Post-sexual abuse trauma: data implications for clinical practice', *Journal of Interpersonal Violence*, vol 2, pp 367–79.

Bryant, R. (1973) 'Professionals in the firing line', *British Journal of Social Work*, vol 3, pp 161–74.

Burchell, B.J., Dat, D., Hudson, M., Lapido, D., Mankelow, R., Nolan, J., Reed, H., Wichert, I.L. and Wilkinson, F. (1999) *Job insecurity and work intensification: Flexibility and the changing boundaries of work*, York: Joseph Rowntree Foundation.

Burman, E. (1996/97) 'False memories, true hopes and the angelic: revenge of the postmodern in therapy', *New Formations*, no 30, winter, pp 122–34.

Burman, E., Aitken, G., Alldred, P., Allwood, R., Billington, T., Goldberg, B., Gordo-Lopez, A.J., Heenan, C., Marks, D. and Warner, S. (1996) *Psychology discourse practice: From regulation to resistance*, London: Taylor and Francis.

Busfield, J. (1996) 'Professionals, the state and the development of mental health policy', in T. Heller, J. Reynolds, R. Gomm, R. Muston and S. Pattison (eds) *Mental health matters: A reader*, London: Macmillan.

Butrym, Z.T. (1976) *The nature of social work*, London: Macmillan.

Cahill, C., Llewelyn, S.P. and Pearson, C. (1991) 'Long term aspects of sexual abuse which occurred in childhood: a review', *British Journal of Clinical Psychology*, vol 30, pp 117–30.

Cameron, D. (1995) *Verbal hygiene*, London: Routledge.

Carey, J. (1992) *The intellectuals and the masses: Pride and prejudice among the literary intelligentsia, 1880–1939*, London: Faber and Faber.

Carson, G. (2006) 'Over 400 social workers referred to the GSCC for alleged misconduct', 17 May, www.communitycare.co.uk.

Caughey, J. (1996) 'Psychological distress in staff of a social services district office: a pilot study', *British Journal of Social Work*, vol 26, pp 389–98.

CCETSW (Central Council for Education and Training in Social Work) (1975) *Education and training for social work*, London: CCETSW.

CCETSW (1989a) *Regulations and guidelines for the approval of agencies and accreditation and training of practice teachers*, London: CCETSW.

CCETSW (1989b) *Rules and requirements for the Diploma in Social Work (Paper 30)*, London: CCETSW.

CCETSW (1991) *One small step towards racial justice (the teaching of anti-racist social work in Diploma in Social Work programmes)*, London: CCETSW.

CCETSW (1995) *Assuring quality in the Diploma in Social Work: Rules and requirements for the Diploma in Social Work (Revised paper 30)*, London: CCETSW.

Chandler, D. (2002) *From Kosovo to Kabul: Human rights and international intervention*, London: Pluto Press.

Clifton, J. and Serdar, H. (2000) *Bully off: Recognising and tackling workplace bullying*, Lyme Regis: Russell House.

Cohen, J.L. (1997) 'Rethinking privacy: the abortion controversy', in J. Weintraub and K. Kumar (eds) *Public and private in thought and practice: Perspectives on a grand dichotomy*, Chicago: University of Chicago Press.

Cohen, S. (2001) *Immigration controls, the family and the welfare state*, London: Jessica Kingsley.

Cohen, S. (2003) *No one is illegal*, Stoke-on-Trent: Trentham Books.

Cohen, S. (2004) 'Breaking the links and pulling the plug', in D. Hayes and B. Humphries (eds) *Social work, immigration and asylum: Debates, dilemmas and ethical issues for social work and social care practice*, London: Jessica Kingsley.

Collett, J. (2004) 'Immigration is a social work issue', in D. Hayes and B. Humphries (eds) *Social work, immigration and asylum: Debates, dilemmas and ethical issues for social work and social care practice*, London: Jessica Kingsley.

Collings, J. and Murray, P. (1996) 'Predictors of stress among social workers: an empirical study', *British Journal of Social Work*, vol 26, pp 357–75.

Collins, S. (2001) 'Bullying in social work organisations', *Practice*, vol 13, no 3, pp 29–44.

Collins, S. and Parry-Jones, B. (2000) 'Stress: the perceptions of social work lecturers in Britain', *British Journal of Social Work*, vol 30, pp 769–94.

Collins, S., Gutridge, P., James, A., Lyn, E. and Williams, C. (2000) 'Racism and anti-racism in placement reports', *Social Work Education*, vol 19, no 1, pp 29–43.

Cooper, D. (1967) *Psychiatry and anti-psychiatry*, London: Tavistock.

Cooper, C. and Cartwright, S. (1994) 'Stress-management interventions in the workplace: stress counselling and stress audits', *British Journal of Guidance and Counselling*, vol 22, pp 65–73.

Cornwall (2005) 'Cornwall County Council – Specialist social work', www.cornwall.gov.uk.

Corrigan, P. and Leonard, P. (1978) *Social work practice under capitalism: A Marxist approach*, London: Macmillan.

Cowen, H. (1999) *Community care, ideology and social policy*, London: Prentice-Hall.

Crichton, J. (1999) 'Mental disorder and crime: coincidence, correlation and cause', *Journal of Forensic Psychiatry*, vol 10, no 3, pp 659–78.

CST (Care Standards Tribunal) (2006) 'YD v the General Social Care Council', www.carestandardstribunal.gov.uk.

CST (2007) 'Hensley Hollingsworth v the General Social Care Council', www.carestandardstribunal.gov.uk.

Dalrymple, J. and Burke, B. (1995) *Anti-oppressive practice: Social care and the law*, Buckingham: Open University Press.

Davies, M. (1981) *The essential social worker: A guide to positive practice*, London: Heinemann Educational.

Davies, R. (ed) (1998) *Stress in social work*, London: Jessica Kingsley.

Davis, A. (1996) 'Risk work and mental health', in H. Kemshall and J. Pritchard *Good practice in risk assessment and risk management*, London: Jessica Kingsley.

Denney, D. (1998) *Social policy and social work*, Oxford: Clarendon Press.

Dent, H. (1999) 'PC pathway to positive action', in T. Philpott (ed) *Political correctness and social work*, London: IEA Health and Welfare Unit.

DfEE (Department for Education and Employment) (1999) *National healthy school standard. Guidance*, London: DfEE.

DfES (Department for Education and Skills) (2000) *Bullying: Don't suffer in silence*, London: DfES.

DH (Department of Health) (1990) *The care programme approach for people with a mental illness referred to the specialist psychiatric services*, HC(90)23, LASSL(90)11, London: DH.

DH (1994) *Introduction of supervision registers for mentally ill people from 1 April 1994*, HSG (94)5, London: DH, Health Service Guidelines.

DH (1995) *Child protection: Messages from research*, London: DH.

DH (1998a) *In-patients formally detained in hospitals under the Mental Health Act 1983 and other legislation in England: 1987–88, 1992–93 and 1997–98*, London: DH.

DH (1998b) *Modernising social services: Promoting independence, improving protection, raising standards*, London: DH.

DH (1999) *National service framework for mental health*, London: Department of Health.

DH (2000a) (Department of Health) *Attitudes to mental illness: Summary report*, London: DH.

DH (2000b) *Care Standards Act 2000*, London: DH.

DH (2000c) *NHS plan*, London: Department of Health.

DH (2000d) *No secrets: Guidance on developing and implementing multi-agency policies and procedures to protect vulnerable adults from abuse*, London: DH.

DH (2000e) *Reforming the Mental Health Act 1983*, London: DH.

DH (2001a) *A safer place: National task force on violence against social care staff*, London: DH.

DH (2001b) *Safety first: Report of the National Confidential Inquiry into suicide and homicide by people with mental illness*, London: DH.

DH (2001c) 'Social work recruitment drive set to be a success', reference number 2001/0645, www.doh.gov.uk.

DH (2002a) Draft Mental Health Bill, London: DH.

DH (2002b) *Requirements for social work training*, London: DH.

DH (2004) Draft Mental Health Bill, London: DH.

DH (2006) Draft Mental Health Bill, London: DH.

DH (2007) *Mental Health Act*, London: DH.

DHSS (Department of Health and Social Security) (1972) *Report of the Committee of Inquiry into Whittingham Hospital*, London: HMSO.

DHSS (1974) *Report of the Committee of Inquiry into the care and supervision provided in relation to Maria Colwell*, London: HMSO.

DHSS (1980) *Report of the Review of Rampton Hospital*, London: HMSO.

DHSS (1988) *Report of the inquiry into child abuse in Cleveland*, London: HMSO.

Dineen, T. (1999) *Manufacturing victims*, London: Constable.

Dominelli, L. (1988) *Anti-racist social work*, London: Macmillan.

Dominelli, L. (1996) 'Deprofessionalizing social work: anti-oppressive practice, competences and postmodernism', *British Journal of Social Work*, vol 25, pp 153–75.

Dominelli, L. (1998) 'Anti-oppressive practice in context', in R. Adams, L. Dominelli and M. Payne (eds) *Social work: Themes, issues and critical debates*, Basingstoke: Macmillan.

Dominelli, L. (2002) *Anti-oppressive social work theory and practice*, Hampshire: Palgrave.

Douglas, M. (1992) *Risk and blame: Essays in cultural theory*, London: Routledge.

Doyle, C. (1997) 'Protection studies: challenging oppression and discrimination', *Social Work Education*, vol 16, no 2, pp 8–19.

DRC (Disability Rights Commission) (2007) *Maintaining standards: Promoting equality*, London: DRC.

Dworkin, A. (1981) *Pornography: Men possessing women*, London: Women's Press.

Dyer, C. (2001) 'We're racist, admits prosecution service chief', *Guardian*, 27 July.

Eastman, N. (1997) 'The Mental Health (Patients in the Community) Act 1995: A critical analysis', *British Journal of Psychiatry*, vol 170, pp 492–6.

Eatock, J. (2000) 'Counselling in primary care: past, present and future', *British Journal of Guidance and Counselling*, vol 28, pp 161–73.

Engels, F. (2005) *The condition of the working class in England*, London: Penguin (first published in English in 1887).

Fairchilds, C.C. (1976) *Poverty and charity in Aix-en-Provence 1640–1789*, Baltimore: Johns Hopkins University Press.

Fawcett, B. and Featherstone, B. (2000) 'Setting the scene: an appraisal of notions of postmodernism, postmodernity and postmodern feminism', in B. Fawcett, B. Featherstone, J. Fook and A. Rossiter (eds) *Practice and research in social work: Postmodern feminist perspectives*, London: Routledge.

Fawcett, B., Featherstone, B., Fook, J. and Rossiter, A. (eds) (2000) *Practice and research in social work: Postmodern feminist perspectives*, London: Routledge.

Field, F. (2003) *Neighbours from hell: The politics of behaviour*, London: Politcos.

Field, T. (1996) *Bullying in sight: How to predict, resist, challenge and combat workplace bullying*, Didcot: Success Unlimited.

Flint, J. (2004) *The responsible tenant: Housing governance and the politics of behaviour*, CNR paper 30, www.bristol.ac.uk/sps/cnrpaperspdf/cnr20pap.pdf

Foucault, M. (1967) *Madness and civilisation: A history of insanity in the age of reason*, London: Tavistock.

Francis, E. (1991) 'Mental health, anti-racism and social work training', in CCETSW (Central Council for Education and Training in Social Work) *One small step towards racial justice (the teaching of anti-racist social work in Diploma in Social Work programmes)*, London: CCETSW.

Furedi, F. (1997) *Culture of fear: Risk-taking and the morality of low expectation*, London: Cassell.

Furedi, F. (2001) *Paranoid parenting: Abandon your anxieties and be a good parent*, London: Penguin.

Furedi, F. (2004) *Therapy culture: Cultivating vulnerability in an uncertain age*, London: Routledge.

Gargett, E. (1977) *The administration of transition: African urban settlement in Rhodesia*, Gwelo: Mambo Press.

Gibson, F., McGrath, A. and Reid, N. (1989) 'Occupational stress in social work', *British Journal of Social Work*, vol 19, pp 1–16.

Giddens, A. (1990) *The consequences of modernity*, Cambridge: Polity Press.

Giddens, A. (1991) *Modernity and self identity*, Cambridge: Polity Press.

Giddens, A. (2000) *The third way and its critics*, Cambridge: Polity Press.

Gilroy, P. (1987) *There ain't no black in the Union Jack: The cultural politics of race and nation*, London: Hutchinson.

Goffman, E. (1959) *The presentation of the self in everyday life*, New York: Doubleday Anchor.

Goffman, E. (1961) *Asylums*, Harmondsworth: Penguin.

Goffman, E. (1963) *Stigma*, Harmondsworth: Penguin.

Graham, P.J. (1971) 'Some aspects of the relationship of social work to behaviour therapy', *British Journal of Social Work*, vol 1, pp 197–208.

Greenwood, E. (1957) 'Attributes of a profession', *Social Work*, vol 2, pp 45–55.

Gregson, O. and Looker, T. (2004) *MMU guide to managing stress*, Manchester: Manchester Metropolitan University.

GSCC (General Social Care Council) (2001) *The post-qualifying handbook: Guidance on awards within the post-qualifying framework*, London: GSCC.

GSCC (2002) *Codes of practice for social care workers and employers*, London: GSCC.

GSCC (2003a) 'Numbers boost to social work education and training', 24 November, www.gscc.org.

GSCC (2003b) 'Regulation of the social care workforce by the GSCC', Briefing note prepared by the General Social Care Council and the Youth Justice Board, www.gscc.org, August.

GSCC (2006) *Specialist standards and requirements for post-qualification social work education and training: Social work in mental health services*, London: GSCC.

GWC (General Whitley Council) (2000) 'Equal Opportunities Agreement', advance letter (GC)1/2000, London: Department of Health.

Hall, S., Critcher, C., Jefferson, T., Clarke, J. and Roberts, B. (1978) *Policing the crisis: Mugging, the state and law and order*, Hampshire: Macmillan.

Halmos, P. (1965) *The faith of the counsellors*, London: Constable.

Hamilton, G. (1940) *The theory and practice of social casework*, New York: Columbia University Press.

Hamilton, G. (1951) *The theory and practice of social casework* (2nd edn), New York: Columbia University Press.

Harding, S. (ed) (1987) *Feminism and methodology*, Indiana: Indiana University Press.

Harding, S. (1991) *Whose science? Whose knowledge: Thinking from women's lives*, Milton Keynes: Open University Press.

Harris, N. (2002) 'Neuroleptic drugs and their management', in N. Harris, S. Williams and T. Bradshaw (eds) *Psychosocial interventions for people with schizophrenia: A practical guide for mental health workers*, Hampshire: Palgrave.

Hartsock, N.C.M. (1987) 'The feminist standpoint: developing the ground for a specifically feminist historical materialism', in S. Harding (ed) *Feminism and methodology*, Indiana: Indiana University Press.

Hartsock, N.C.M. (1998) *The feminist standpoint revisited and other essays*, Oxford: Westview Press.

Hayes, D. (2002) 'From aliens to asylum seekers: a history of immigration controls and welfare', in S. Cohen, B. Humphries and E. Mynott (eds) *From immigration control to welfare control*, London: Routledge.

Hayes, D. (2005) 'Social work with asylum seekers', in R. Adams, L. Dominelli and M. Payne (eds) *Social work futures: Crossing boundaries, transforming practice*, Hampshire: Palgrave.

Hayes, D. and Humphries, B. (eds) (2004) *Social work, immigration and asylum: Debates, dilemmas and ethical issues for social work and social care practice*, London: Jessica Kingsley.

Heartfield, J. (2002) *The 'death of the subject' explained*, Sheffield: Sheffield Hallam University Press.

Hehir, B. (2004) 'The pregnancy police', 3 November, www.spiked-online.com.

Hiday, V. (1995) 'The social context of mental illness and violence', *Journal of Health and Social Behaviour*, vol 36, June, pp 122–37.

Hillyard, P. and Percy-Smith, J. (1988) *The coercive state: The decline of democracy in Britain*, London: Fontana.

Hodgson, L. (2004) 'Manufactured civil society: counting the cost', *Critical Social Policy*, vol 24, no 2, pp 139–64.

Hollis, F. (1970) 'The psychosocial approach to the practice of casework', in R.W. Roberts and R.H. Nees (eds) *Theories of social casework*, Chicago: Chicago University Press.

Home Office (2004) *Tackling domestic violence: The role of health professionals* (2nd edn), London: Home Office.

Horner, N. (2003) *What is social work? Context and perspectives*, Exeter: Learning Matters.

Horton, R. (2003) 'Medical journals: evidence of bias against the diseases of poverty', *Lancet*, no 361, pp 712–13.

House, R. (1997) 'Training: a guarantee of competence?', in R. House and N. Totton (eds) *Implausible professions: Arguments for pluralism and autonomy in psychotherapy and counselling*, Ross-on-Wye: PCSS Books.

Howlett, M. (1997) 'Community care homicide inquiries and risk assessment', in H. Kemshall and J. Pritchard (eds) *Good practice in risk assessment and risk management 2*, London: Jessica Kingsley.

Hudson, K. (1971) 'Some social and emotional implications of dependence on machinery', *British Journal of Social Work*, vol 1, no 2, pp 173–95.

Hume, M. (2003) 'The phoney moral crusade against racism', 24 October, www.spiked-online.com.

Humphries, B. (1997) 'Reading social work: competing discourses in the rules and requirements for the Diploma in Social Work', *British Journal of Social Work*, vol 27, pp 641–58.

Humphries, B. (2004) 'An unacceptable role for social work: implementing immigration policy', *British Journal of Social Work*, vol 34, pp 93–107.

Humphries, B. and Mynott, E. (2001) *Living your life across boundaries: Young separated refugees in Greater Manchester*, Manchester: Save the Children.

Huntingdon, A. (1998) 'When the professional is personal: issues of identity and practice', *Practice*, vol 10, no 1, pp 5–14.

Ife, J. (1997) *Rethinking social work*, Melbourne: Longman.

Irvine, E. (1978) 'Psychiatric social work: training for psychiatric social work', in E. Younghusband (ed) *Social work in Britain 1950–1975: A follow-up study*, London: George Allen and Unwin.

Jacoby, R. (1999) *The end of utopia: Culture and politics in an age of apathy*, New York: Basic Books.

James, O. (1997) *Britain on the couch*, London: Century.

James, O. (2005) 'Think again', *Guardian*, 22 October.

Jansen, J. (1971) 'Freedom of thought in social work', *Social Work Today*, vol 2, no 20, pp 3–4.

Johnson, L.C. (1983) *Social work practice: A generalist approach*, Massachusetts: Allyn and Bacon.

Johnstone, L. (2000) *Users and abusers of psychiatry* (2nd edn), London: Routledge.

Jones, C. (1983) *State social work and the working class*, London: Macmillan.

Jones, C. (1997) 'Poverty', in M. Davies (ed) *The Blackwell companion to social work*, Oxford: Blackwell.

Jones, C., Ferguson, I., Lavalette, M. and Penketh, L. (2004) 'Social work and social justice: a manifesto for a new engaged practice', www.liv.ac.uk/ssp/Social_Work_Manifesto.html.

Jones, L. (1996) 'The madness of George III', in T. Heller, J. Reynolds, R. Gomm, R. Muston and S. Pattison (eds) *Mental health matters: A reader*, London: Macmillan.

Jordan, B. (1984) *Invitation to social work*, Oxford: Martin Robertson.

Jordan, B. (1998) *The new politics of welfare*, London: Sage.

Jordan, B. and Parton, N. (1983) *The political dimensions of social work*, Oxford: Basil Blackwell.

Kempe, C.H., Silverman, F.N., Steel, B.F., Droegmueller, W. and Silver, H.K. (1962) 'The battered child syndrome', *Journal of the American Medical Association*, vol 181, pp 17–24.

Kemshall, H. and Pritchard, J. (1996) *Good practice in risk assessment and risk management*, London: Jessica Kingsley.

Kenny, C. (2007) 'Practise what we preach', *Community Care*, 23 August, pp 16–17.

Khan, P. (2000) 'Asylum seekers in the UK: implications for social service involvement', *Social Work and Social Sciences Review*, vol 8, no 2, pp 116–29.

Kutek, A. (1998) 'No health, no service', in R. Davies (ed) *Stress in social work*, London: Jessica Kingsley.

Ladyman, S. (2003) 'Universities to receive extra £1.28 million to boost social work education', 12 September, www.gscc.org.uk/News+and+events/Media+releases/2003+archive/Universities.

Langan, M. (2002) 'The legacy of radical social work', in R. Adams, L. Dominelli and M. Payne (eds) *Social work: Themes, issues and critical debates*, Hampshire: Palgrave.

Langan, M. and Day, L. (1992) *Women, social work and oppression: Issues in anti-discriminatory practice*, London: Routledge.

Langan, M. and Lee, P. (1989) 'Whatever happened to radical social work?', in M. Langan and P. Lee (eds) *Radical social work today*, London: Unwin Hyman.

Laurance, J. (2003) *Pure madness: How fear drives the mental health system*, London: Routledge.

Layard, R. (2005) 'Happiness is back', *Prospect*, no 108, March.

Laybourn, K. (1995) *The evolution of British social policy and the welfare state 1800–1993*, Keele: Keele University Press.

Leason, K. (2006) 'When the mask slips', *Community Care*, 18–24 May.

Lees, R. (1972) *Politics and social work*, London: Routledge and Kegan-Paul.

Levi, M., Burrows, J., Fleming, M.H. and Hopkins, M. (2007) *The nature, extent and economic impact of fraud in the UK*, Report for the Association of Chief Police Officers Economic Crime Portfolio, London: ACPO.

Levitas, R. (1998) *The inclusive society: Social exclusion and New Labour*, Hampshire: Palgrave.

Levy, A. and Kahan, B. (1991) *The Pindown experience and the protection of children: The report of the Staffordshire child care inquiry*, Stafford: Staffordshire County Council.

Lister, R. (ed) (1996) *Charles Murray and the underclass: The developing debate*, London: Institute of Economic Affairs.

Lloyd, M. (2002) 'Care management', in R. Adams, L. Dominelli and M. Payne (eds) *Critical practice in social work*, Hampshire: Palgrave.

Lorenz, W. (1994) *Social work in a changing Europe*, London: Routledge.

Lurie, H.L. (1935) 'Re-examination of child welfare functions in family and foster care agencies', in F. Lowry (ed) (1939) *Readings in social casework 1920–1938: Selected responses for the casework practitioner*, New York: Columbia University Press.

Lyotard, J.F. (1989) *The postmodern condition: A report on knowledge*, Manchester: Manchester University Press.

McCann, G. and McKeown, M. (2002) 'Risk and serious mental health issues', in N. Harris, S. Williams and T. Bradshaw (eds) *Psychosocial interventions for people with schizophrenia*, Hampshire: Palgrave.

McDonald, N. and Doyle, M. (1981) *The stresses of work: Health and safety in the workplace*, Surrey: Thomas Nelson.

McGuire, J. and Priestly, P. (1985) *Offending behaviour: Skills and stratagems for going straight*, London: Batsford.

McKenzie, K. (1999) 'Something borrowed from the blues', *British Medical Journal*, no 318, pp 616–17.

McLaughlin, K. (2006) 'Scare in the community', 6 December, www.spiked-online.co.uk.

McLaughlin, K. (2007) 'Revisiting the public/private divide: theoretical, political and personal implications of their unification', *Practice*, vol 19, no 4, pp 241–53.

McLean, J. (1999) 'Satisfaction, stress and control over work', in S. Balloch, J. McLean and M. Fisher (eds) *Social services: Working under pressure*, Bristol: The Policy Press.

Macey, M. and Moxon, E. (1996) 'An examination of anti-racist and anti-oppressive theory and practice in social work education', *British Journal of Social Work*, vol 26, pp 297–314.

Macpherson, W. (1999) *The Stephen Lawrence Inquiry: Report of an inquiry by Sir William Macpherson of Cluny*, London: HMSO.

Malherbe, M. (1980) *Accreditation in social work: Principles and Issues in context: A contribution to the debate* (CCETSW Study 4), London: CCETSW.

Malik, K. (1996) *The meaning of race*, London: Macmillan.

Malik, K. (2005) 'The Islamophobia myth', www.kenanmalik.com/essays/islamophobia_prospect.html

Manktelow, R. (1999) 'The 1986 Mental Health (N.I.) Order and approved social work in Northern Ireland: time for change', *Practice*, vol 11, no 1, pp 23–34.

Marin, M. (1996) 'Claims that could damage a nation's health', *Daily Telegraph*, 5 December.

Melhuish, E., Belsky, J. and Leyland, A. (2004) *The impact of Sure Start local programmes on child development and family functioning: A report on preliminary findings*, London: Birkbeck University.

MHAC (Mental Health Act Commission) (1999) *Eighth biennial report: 1997–1999*, London: The Stationery Office.

MHF (Mental Health Foundation) (1999) *The big picture*, London: MHF.

Middleton, D. and Edwards, D. (eds) (1991) *Collective remembering*, London: Sage.

Miles, A. (1981) *The mentally ill in contemporary society: A sociological introduction*, Oxford: Robertson.

MMU (Manchester Metropolitan University) (2007) *Placement handbook: Guidelines for students and practice teachers*, Manchester: Department of Social Work, MMU.

Molyneux, J. (1993) 'The politically correct controversy', *International Socialism*, no 61, pp 43–74.

Mullender, A. (1995) 'The assessment of anti-oppressive practice in the diploma in social work', *Issues in Social Work Education*, vol 15, no 1, pp 67–77.

Mullender, A. (2002) 'Persistent oppressions: the example of domestic violence', in R. Adams, L. Dominelli and M. Payne (eds) *Critical practice in social work*, Hampshire: Palgrave.

Mullender, A. (2003) 'Foreword', in N. Thompson *Promoting equality: Challenging discrimination and oppression*, Basingstoke: Palgrave.

Newton, T. (1999) 'Stress discourse and individualization', in C. Feltham (ed) *Controversies in psychotherapy and counselling*, London: Sage.

Nolan, J.L. (1998) *The therapeutic state: Justifying government at century's end*, New York: New York University Press.

Oliver, C. and Candappa, M. (2003) *Tackling bullying: Listening to the views of children and young people* (summary report), London: Institute of Education.

Oliver, M. (1990) *The politics of disablement: A sociological approach*, London: Macmillan.

Orr, M. (1999) 'Believing patients', in C. Feltham (ed) *Controversies in psychotherapy and counselling*, London: Sage.

Parker, C. and McCulloch, A. (1999) *Key issues from homicide inquiries*, London: MIND.

Parker, I. (1989) 'Discourse and power', in J. Shotter and K.J. Gergen (eds) *Texts of identity*, London: Sage.

Parker, I. (2002) *Critical discursive psychology*, London: Palgrave.

Parker, I. (2005) *Qualitative psychology: Introducing radical research*, Maidenhead: Open University Press.

Parker, I., Georgaca, E., Harper, D., McLaughlin, T. and Stowell, M.S. (1995) *Deconstructing psychopathology*, London: Sage.

Parker, J., Hillison, K. and Wilson, L. (2003) 'SWiSP: the social work students in schools project', *Practice*, vol 15, no 4, pp 69–87.

Parry Jones, W.L. (1972) *The trade in lunacy*, London: Routledge and Kegan-Paul.

Parton, N. (1985) *The politics of child abuse*, Basingstoke: Macmillan.

Parton, N. (1988) 'Risk, advanced liberalism and child welfare: the need to rediscover uncertainty and ambiguity', *British Journal of Social Work*, vol 28, no 1, pp 5–27.

Parton, N. (1989) 'Child abuse', in B. Kahan (ed) *Child care research: Policy and practice*, London: Hodder and Stoughton.

Parton, N. (1994) 'Problematics of government: (post) modernity and social work', *British Journal of Social Work*, vol 24, pp 9–32.

Parton, N. and O'Byrne, P. (2000) *Constructive social work: Towards a new practice*, Basingstoke: Palgrave.

Parton, N., Thorpe, D. and Wattam, C. (1997) *Child protection: Risk and the moral order*, Basingstoke: Macmillan.

Patmore, A. (2006) *The truth about stress*, London: Atlantic Books.

Payne, M. (1996) *What is professional social work?*, Birmingham: Venture Press.

Payne, M. (1997) *Modern social work theory* (2nd edn), London: Macmillan.

Payne, M. (2002) 'The role and achievement of a professional association in the late twentieth century: the British Association of Social Workers 1970–2000', *British Journal of Social Work*, vol 32, pp 969–95.

Payne, M. (2005) *The origins of social work: Continuity and change*, Hampshire: Palgrave.

Payne, M. (2006) *What is professional social work*, (2nd edn), Bristol: The Policy Press.

Pearson, G. (1975) 'Making good social workers: bad promises and good omens', in R. Bailey and M. Brake (eds) *Radical social work*, London: Edward Arnold.

Pearson, G., Treseder, J. and Yelloly, M. (eds) (1988) *Social work and the legacy of Freud: Psychoanalysis and its uses*, Hampshire: Macmillan.

Penketh, L. (1998) 'Anti-racist policies and practice: the case of CCETSW's Paper 30', in M. Lavalette and L. Penketh (eds) *Anti-racism and social welfare*, Aldershot: Ashgate.

Penketh, L. (2000) *Tackling institutional racism: Anti-racist policies and social work education and training*, Bristol: The Policy Press.

Perry, R.W. (2004) 'The impact of criminal conviction disclosure on the self-reported offending profile of social work', *British Journal of Social Work*, vol 34, pp 997–1008.

Phillips, M. (1994) 'Illiberal liberalism', in S. Dunant (ed) *The war of the words: The political correctness debate*, London: Virago.

Phillipson, J. (1992) *Practising equality: Women, men and social work*, London: CCETSW.

Philo, G., Platt, S., Henderson, L., McLaughlin, G. and Burnside, J. (1996) 'Media images of mental distress', in T. Heller, J. Reynolds, R. Gomm, R. Muston and S. Pattison (eds) *Mental health matters: A reader*, London: Macmillan.

Philpot, T. (1999) 'Editor's introduction: the modern mark of Cain', in T. Philpot (ed) *Political correctness and social work*, London: IEA Health and Welfare Unit.

Pierson, J. (1999) 'Social work and civil society', in T. Philpott (ed) *Political correctness and social work*, London: IEA Health and Welfare Unit.

Pilgrim, D. and Rogers, A. (1996) 'Two notions of risk in mental health debates', in T. Heller, J. Reynolds, R. Gomm, R. Muston and S. Pattison (eds) *Mental health matters: A reader*, London: Macmillan.

Pinker, R. (1993) 'A lethal kind of looniness', *Times Higher Educational Supplement*, 10 September.

Pinker, R. (1999) 'Social work and adoption: a case of mistaken identities', in T. Philpot (ed) *Political correctness and social work*, London, IEA Health and Welfare Unit.

Popplestone, G. (1971) 'Ideology of professional community workers', *British Journal of Social Work*, vol 1, pp 85–104.

Powell, F. (2001) *The politics of social work*, London: Sage.

Preston-Shoot, M. (1995) 'Assessing anti-oppressive practice', *Social Work Education*, vol 14, no 2, pp 11–29.

Pringle, M. and Laverty, J. (1993) 'A counsellor in every practice', *British Medical Journal*, no 306, pp 2–3.

Prins, H. (1999) *Will they do it again? Risk assessment and management in criminal justice and psychiatry*, London: Routledge.

Pupavac, V. (2001) 'Therapeutic governance: psycho-social intervention and trauma risk management', *Disasters*, vol 25, no 4, pp 358–72.

Randall, P. and Parker, J. (2000) 'Bullying', in M. Davies (ed) *The encyclopaedia of social work*, Oxford: Blackwell.

Rankin, G. (1970) 'Professional social work and the campaign against poverty', *Social Work Today*, vol 1, no 10, pp 19–21.

Rayner, C. (1997) 'The incidence of workplace bullying', *Journal of Community and Applied Social Psychology*, vol 7, pp 199–208.

Read, J. (1997) 'Child abuse and psychosis: a literature review and implications for professional practice', *Professional Psychology: Research and Practice*, no 28, pp 448–56.

Read, J. (1998) 'Child abuse and severity of disturbance among adult psychiatric inpatients', *Child Abuse and Neglect*, vol 22, pp 359–68.

Rees, G. and Stein, M. (1999) *The abuse of adolescents within the family*, London: NSPCC.

Rein, M. (1970) 'Social work in search of a radical profession', *Social Work*, vol 15, no 2, pp 13–28.

Richardson, P. (1997) 'ABC of mental health: psychological problems', *British Medical Journal*, no 315, pp 733–5.

Richmond, M. (1917) *Social diagnosis*, New York: Russell Sage.

Richmond, M. (1922) *What is social casework?*, New York: Russell Sage.

Rickford, F. (1999) 'Stressed out', *Community Care*, 26 August–1 September, pp 22–3.

Rieff, P. (1966) *The triumph of the therapeutic: Uses of faith after Freud*, New York: Harper.

Ritchie, J., Dick, D. and Lingham, R. (1994) *The report of the inquiry into the care and treatment of Christopher Clunis*, London: HMSO.

Robinson, D. (1996) 'Developing risk assessment scales in forensic psychiatry', *Psychiatric Care*, vol 3, no 4, pp 146–52.

Romme, M.A.J. and Escher, A.D.M.A.C. (1993) (eds) *Accepting voices*, London: MIND.

Romme, M.A.J., Honig, A., Noorthoorn, E.O. and Escher, A.D.M.A.C. (1992) 'Coping with hearing voices: an emancipatory approach', *British Journal of Psychiatry*, no 161, pp 99–103.

Rose, N. (1985) *The psychological complex: Psychology, politics and society in England, 1869–1939*, London: Routledge and Kegan Paul.

Rose, N. (1990) *Governing the soul: The shaping of the private self*, London: Routledge.

Ryan, T. (1996) 'Risk management and people with mental health problems', in H. Kemshall and J. Pritchard (eds) *Good practice in risk assessment and risk management, Volume 1*, London: Jessica Kingsley.

Sandeman, J. (2006) 'The battle of the lunchbox', 12 December, www.spiked-online.com.

Sarbin, T.R. (1990) 'Towards the obsolescence of schizophrenia', *Journal of Mind and Behaviour*, vol 11, pp 259–83.

Scheff, T. (1984) *Being mentally ill: A sociological theory* (2nd edn), Chicago: Aldine.

Schneider, K. (1959) *Clinical psychopathology*, New York: Grune and Stratton.

Scotford, R. (1999) 'False memories: a peripheral issue', in C. Feltham (ed) *Controversies in psychotherapy and counselling*, London: Sage.

Scottish Office (1992) *The report of the inquiry into the removal of children from Orkney in February 1991*, Edinburgh: HMSO.

Scull, A. (1984) *Decarceration* (2nd edn), Cambridge: Polity Press.

Sedgwick, P. (1982) *Psycho politics*, London: Pluto Press.

Seed, P. (1973) *The expansion of social work in Britain*, London: Routledge and Kegan-Paul.

Sheppard, M. (1990) *Mental health: The role of the approved social worker*, Sheffield: Joint Unit for the Social Services Research Monographs, Research in Practice Series, University of Sheffield.

Showalter, E. (1997) *Hystories: Hysterical epidemics and modern culture*, New York: Columbia University Press.

Singh, G. (1996) 'Promoting anti-racist and black perspectives in social work education and practice teaching', *Social Work Education*, vol 15, no 2, pp 35–56.

Singh, G. (2002) 'The political challenge of anti-racism in social care and health', in D.R. Tomlinson and W. Trew (eds) *Equalising opportunities, minimising oppression: A critical review of anti-discriminatory policies in health and social welfare*, London: Routledge.

Sivanandan, A. (1985) 'RAT and the degradation of black struggle', *Race and Class*, vol 26, no 4, pp 1–33.

Skellington, R. (1996) *Race in Britain today* (2nd edn), London: Sage.

Skinner, B. F. (1971) *Beyond freedom and dignity*, Indianapolis: Hackett.

Slater, P. (2004) 'Reforming professional training and protecting vulnerable adults from abuse: a thematic analysis of the new social work degree's prescribed curriculum', *British Journal of Social Work*, vol 34, pp 649–61.

Smail, D. (2001) *The origins of unhappiness: A new understanding of personal distress*, London: Robinson.

SSI (Social Services Inspectorate) (1993) *No longer afraid*, SSI guidelines, London: HMSO.

Stanley, L. and Wise, S. (1993) *Breaking out again*, London: Routledge.

Steadman, H., Mulvey, E.P., Monahan, J., Robbins, P.C., Appelbaum, P.S., Grisso, T., Roth, L.H. and Silver, E. (1998) 'Violence by people discharged from acute psychiatric inpatient facilities and by others in the same neighbourhood', *Archives of General Psychiatry*, vol 55, pp 1–9.

Steele, L. (1998) 'Mind games', *Community Care*, 3–9 December, pp 22–3.

Stevens, T. (1999) *Bullying and sexual harassment*, London: Institute of Personnel and Development.

Stone Report (2006) *Report of the independent inquiry into the care and treatment of Michael Stone*, Maidstone: South East Coast Strategic Health Authority, Kent County Council and Kent Probation Area.

Stroud, J. and Pritchard, C. (2001) 'Child homicide. Psychiatric disorder and dangerousness: a review and an empirical approach', *British Journal of Social Work*, vol 31, pp 249–69.

Sunderland (2005) 'Sunderland City Council Education Social Work Service', www.sunderland.gov.uk.

Swanson, J.W., Holzer, C.E., Ganju, V.K. and Jono, R.T. (1990) 'Violence and psychiatric disorder in the community: evidence from the epidemologic catchment area surveys', *Hospital and Community Psychiatry*, no 41, pp 761–70.

Syal, M. (1994) 'PC: GLC', in S. Dunant (ed) *The war of the words: The political correctness controversy*, London: Virago.

Szasz, T.S. (1961) *The myth of mental illness: Foundations of a theory of personal conduct*, New York: Dell.

Szasz, T.S. (1991) *Ideology and insanity: Essays on the psychiatric dehumanization of man*, New York: Syracuse University Press.

Szasz, T.S. (1997) *The manufacture of madness: A comparative study of the inquisition and the mental health movement*, New York: Syracuse University Press (originally published in 1970 by Harper and Row, New York).

Szasz, T.S. (2004) 'What is psychoanalysis?', in A. Casement (ed) *Who owns psychoanalysis?*, London: Karnac.

Taft, J. (ed) (1944) *A functional approach to family casework*, Philadelphia: University of Pennsylvania Press.

Tanner, D. (1998) 'The jeopardy of risk', *Practice*, vol 10, no 1, pp 15–28.

Taylor, P.J. and Gunn, J. (1999) 'Homicides by people with mental illness: myth and reality', *British Journal of Psychiatry*, vol 174, pp 9–14.

Tehrani, N. (2004) 'Bullying: a source of chronic post traumatic stress?', *British Journal of Guidance and Counselling*, vol 32, no 3, pp 357–66.

Thomas, P. (1997) *The dialectics of schizophrenia*, London: Free Association Books.

Thompson, A. (1999) 'Danger zone', *Community Care*, 22–28 July, pp 24-5.

Thompson, N. (1993) *Anti-discriminatory practice*, Hampshire: Macmillan.

Thompson, N. (1994) 'Preface', in N. Thompson, M. Murphy and S. Stradling *Dealing with stress*, Hampshire: Macmillan.

Thompson, N. (2000) *Tackling bullying and harassment in the workplace: A personal guide*, Birmingham: Pepar.

Thompson, N. (2002) *People skills* (2nd edn), Basingstoke: Palgrave.

Thompson, N., Murphy, M. and Stradling, S. (1994) *Dealing with stress*, Hampshire: Macmillan.

Tompson, K. (1988) *Under siege: Racial violence in Britain today*, London: Penguin.

Totton, N. (1997) 'Inputs and outcomes: the medical model and professionalisation', in N. House and N. Totton (eds) *Implausible professions: Arguments for pluralism and autonomy in psychotherapy and counselling*, Ross-on-Wye: PCCS Books.

Turney, D. (1996) *The language of anti-racism in social work: Towards a deconstructive reading*, London: University of London.

Valios, N. (1999) 'Declare war on violence', *Community Care*, 22–28 July, pp 12-13.

Vevers, S. and Taylor, A. (2005) 'Children taken into care due to asylum policy', 31 March, www.communitycare.co.uk.

Wainwright, D. and Calnan, M. (2002) *Work stress: The making of a modern epidemic*, Buckingham: Open University Press.

Walker, N. (1978) 'Dangerous people', *International Journal of Law and Psychiatry*, vol 1, pp 37–50.

Warner, N. (1992) *Choosing with care: The report of the committee of inquiry into the selection, development and management of staff in children's homes*, London: HMSO.

White, M. (1993) 'Deconstruction and therapy', in S. Gilligan and R. Price (eds) *Therapeutic conversations*, New York: Norton.

WHO (World Health Organisation) (1973) *Report of the eighth seminar on the standardisation of psychiatric diagnosis, classification and statistics*, Geneva: WHO.

Wilkes, R. (1981) *Social work with undervalued groups*, London: Tavistock.

Wilmott, C. (1998) 'Public pressure: private stress', in R. Davies (ed) *Stress in social work*, London: Jessica Kingsley.

Winchester, R. (2001) 'Dangerous assumptions', *Community Care*, 22–28 February, pp 20–1.

Wolfe, A. (1997) 'Public and private in theory and practice: some implications of an uncertain boundary', in J. Weintraub and K. Kumar (eds) *Public and private in thought and practice: Perspectives on a grand dichotomy*, Chicago: University of Chicago Press.

Woodrofe, K. (1962) *From charity to social work*, London: Routledge and Kegan Paul.

Wooton, B. (1959) *Social science and social pathology*, London: Allen and Unwin.

Yelloly, M. (1987) 'Why the theory couldn't become practice', *Community Care*, 29 January, pp 18–19.

Younghusband, E. (1970) 'Social work and social work values', *Social Work Today*, vol 1, no 6, pp 5–13.

ZT Monitor (1997) *The Journal of the Zito Trust*, no 2, October.

Index